MW01493391

AN] THE COLLECTION
VOLUME FIVE:
DHARMA & KARMA
(FIVE BOOKS)

DHARMA

KARMA

A STUDY IN KARMA

ELEMENTARY LESSONS ON KARMA

SOME KARMIC PROBLEMS

CONTENTS

THE TIMELESS WISDOM COLLECTION

Emerson once said: *"Consider what you have in the smallest chosen library. A company of the wisest and wittiest men that could be picked out of all civil countries in a thousand years, have set in best order the results of their learning and wisdom. The men themselves were hid and inaccessible, solitary, impatient of interruptions, fenced by etiquette; but the thought which they did not uncover to their bosom friend is here written out in transparent words to us, the strangers of another age."*

TWC is YOUR small library. Thousands of individual books and anthologies, the best of the best in fiction and non-fiction from the 19th and 20th Centuries, written by men and women whose lives were committed to enlighten the world with the wisdom of the ages.

Our fiction features names as Hemingway, Faulkner, Wells, Orwell, Huxley, Doyle, Twain, Burroughs, Chesterton, Alcott, C. S. Lewis, J. M. Barrie, Edgar Wallace, and hundreds more... Authors who have enriched our lives and forever enlarged our capacity to dream, to get enamoured by the characters, to suffer their pain, tragedies, and triumphs as if they were ours; as if they were true...

In self-development and positive-thinking, our authors include Napoleon Hill, Dale Carnegie, Charles Haanel, William Atkinson, Orison Swett Marden, Wallace Wattles, James Allen, Christian D. Larson, Florence Scovell-Shinn, Robert Collier and many more.

In Psychology, we have the works of Freud, Jung, Coué, Coriat, Adler and many others; and in philosophy, the works of Kant, Russell, Whitehead and Eucken, among others. In theosophy and mysticism, our authors include Blavatsky, Bulwer, Besant, Leadbeater, and Sinnet. We feature the works of scientists as Eddington, Darwin, and J.W.Dunne; successful industrialists as Henry Ford, Andrew Carnegie and Charles Schwab; and Economists as John Maynard Keynes...

Thousands of carefully selected masterpieces that have brilliantly captured the essence of life, are now being placed in your hands. *The results of the learning and wisdom of the greatest minds, set in best order,* as Emerson would say. Books for enlightenment, learning, illumination... that will provide the seeker –the one who is ready and is paying attention–, some of the deepest answers to life.

Mauricio Chaves-Mesén, Author of
12 Laws of Successful Entrepreneurs;
Think Success, and *The Knights of Nostradamus*

BOOK ONE
DHARMA

Three Lectures delivered at the Eighth Annual Convention
of the Indian Section of the Theosophical Society,
Held at Varanasi (Benares) on October 25th, 26th and 27th, 1898.

I. DIFFERENCES

WHEN the nations of the earth were sent forth one after the other, a special word was given by God to each, the word which each was to say to the world, the peculiar word from the Eternal which each one was to speak. As we glance over the history of the nations, we can hear resounding from the collective mouth of the people this word, spoken out in action, the contribution of that nation to the ideal and perfect humanity. To Egypt in old days, the word was Religion; to Persia the word was Purity; to Chaldea the word was Science; to Greece the word was Beauty; to Rome the word was Law; and to India, the eldest-born of His children, to India He gave a word that summed up the whole in one, the word Dharma. That is the word of India to the world.

But we cannot speak this word, so full of meaning, so vast in its out-reaching force, without making our bow at the feet of him who is the greatest embodiment of Dharma that the world has ever seen - our bow to Bhishma, the son of Ganga, the mightiest incarnation of Duty. Come with me for a while, traveling five-thousand years back in time, and see this hero, lying on his bed of arrows on the field of Kurukshetra, there holding Death at bay, until the right hour should strike. We pass through heaps upon heaps of the slaughtered warriors, over mountains of dead elephants and horses, and we pass by many a funeral pyre, many a heap of broken weapons and chariots. We come to the hero lying on the bed of arrows, transfixed with hundreds of arrows and his head resting on a pillow of arrows. Far he has rejected the pillows they brought him of soft down, and accepted only the arrowy pillow made by Arjuna. He, perfect in Dharma, had, while still a youth, for the sake of his father, for the sake of the duty that he owed to his father, for the sake of the love he bore to his father, made that great vow of renouncing family life, renouncing the crown, in order that the father's will might be done, and the father's heart be satisfied. And Shantanu gave him his blessing, that wondrous boon, that Death should not come to him until he came at his own command, until he willed to die. When he fell, pierced by hundreds of arrows, the sun has in his southern path, and the season was not favourable for the death of one who was not to return any more. He used the power that his father had given him, and made Death stand aside until the sun should open up the way to eternal peace and liberation. As he lay there for many a weary day, racked with the agonies of his wounds, tortured by the anguish of the mangled body that he wore, there came around him many Rishis and the remnants of the Aryan kings, and thither came also Shri Krishna, to see the faithful one. Thither came the five princes, the sons of Pandu, the victors in the mighty war, and they stood round him weeping and worshipping him, and longing to be taught by him. To him, in the midst of that bitter anguish, came the words from One whose lips were the lips of God, and He released him from the burning fever, and He gave him bodily rest and clearness of mind and quietness of the inner man, and then He bade him teach to the world what Dharma is - he whose whole life had taught it, who had not swerved from the path of righteousness, who whether as son, or prince, or statesman, or warrior, had always trodden the narrow path. He was asked for teaching by those who were around him, and Vasudeva bade him speak of Dharma, because he was fit to teach (*Mahabharata*, Shanti Parva, § LIV).

Then there drew closer round him the sons of Pandu, headed by their eldest brother Yudhishthira, who was the leader of the host that had brought Bhishma to his death; and he was afraid of coming near and asking questions, thinking that as the arrows were really his, being shot for his cause, he was guilty of the blood of his elder, and he ought not to ask to be taught. Seeing his hesitation, Bhishma, whose mind was ever balanced, who had trodden the difficult path of duty without being moved to the right hand or the left, spoke the memorable words: "As the duty of Brahmanas consists in the practice of charity, study, and penance, so the duty of Kshattriyas is to cast away their bodies in battle. A Kshattriya should slay sires and grandsires and brothers and preceptors and relatives and kinsmen, that may engage with him in unjust battle. This is their declared duty. That Kshattriya, O Keshava, is said to be acquainted with his duty who slays in battle his very preceptors, if they happen to be sinful and covetous and disregardful of restraints and vows. . . . . . Ask me, O child, without any anxiety". Then, just as Vasudeva, in speaking of Bhishma, had described Bhishma's right to speak as teacher, so Bhishma himself in turn, in addressing the princes, described the qualities that were needed in those who would ask questions on the problem of Dharma:

"Let the son of Pandu, in whom are intelligence, self-restraint, brahmacharya, forgiveness, righteousness, mental vigor and energy, put questions to me. Let the son of Pandu, who always by his good offices honors his relatives and guests and servants and others that are dependent on him, put questions to me. Let the son of Pandu, in whom are truth and charity and penances, heroism, peacefulness, cleverness and fearlessness, put questions to me." (*Ibid. § LIV.*).

Such are some of the characteristics of the man who may seek to understand the mysteries of Dharma. Such are the qualities which you and I must try to develop, if we are to understand the teachings, if we are to be worthy to enquire.

Then began that wonderful discourse, without parallel among the discourses of the world. It treats of the duties of Kings and of subjects, the duties of the four orders, of the four modes of life, duties for every kind of man, duties distinct from each other and suited to every stage of evolution. Every one of you ought to know that great discourse, ought to study it, not only for its literary beauty, but for its moral grandeur. If we could but follow on the path traced by Bhishma, then would our evolution quicken, then would the day of India's redemption draw nearer to its dawn.

With regard to morality - a subject closely bound up with Dharma, and which cannot be understood without a knowledge of what is meant by Dharma - with regard to morality, some think that it is a simple thing. So it is in its broad outlines. The boundaries of right and wrong in the common actions of life are clear, simple, and definite. For a man of small development, for a man of narrow intelligence, for a man of restricted knowledge, morality seems simple enough. But for those of deep knowledge and high intelligence, for those who are evolving towards the higher grades of humanity, for those who desire to understand its mysteries, for them morality is very difficult: "Morality is very subtle," as the prince Yudhishthira said when he was dealing with the problem of the marriage of Draupadi with the five sons of Pandu. And one greater than that prince had spoken of the difficulty; Shri Krishna, the Avatara, in His discourse delivered on the field of Kurukshetra, spoke on this very question of the difficulty of action. He said:

"What is action, what inaction? Even the wise are hereby perplexed. It is needful to discriminate action, to discriminate unlawful action, to discriminate inaction; mysterious is the path of action" (*Bhagavad Gita*, iv. 16-17.).

Mysterious is the path of action; mysterious, because morality is not, as the simple-minded think, one and the same for all; because it varies with the Dharma of the individual. What is right for one, is wrong for another. And what is wrong for one is right for another. Morality is an individual thing, and it depends upon the Dharma of the man who is acting, and not upon what is sometimes called "absolute right and wrong". There is nothing absolute in a conditioned universe. And right and wrong are relative, and must be judged in relation to the individual and his duties. Thus the greatest of all Teachers said with regard to Dharma - and this will guide us in our tangled path – "Better one's own Dharma, though destitute of merit, than the Dharma of another, well discharged. Better death in the discharge of one's own Dharma; the Dharma of another is full of danger" (*Ibid.* iv. 35.).

He repeated the same thought again at the end of that immortal discourse, and He said - but then changed in such a way as to throw fresh light on the subject: "Better is one's own Dharma, though destitute of merits, than the well executed Dharma of another. He who doeth the Karma laid down by his own nature incurreth not sin" (*Ibid.* xviii. 47.). There He expounds more fully this teaching, and He traces for us one by one the Dharma of the four great castes, and the very wording that He uses shows us the meaning of this word, which is sometimes translated as Duty, sometimes as Law, sometimes as Righteousness, sometimes as Religion. It means these, and more than any of them, for the meaning is deeper and wider than any of thee words expresses. Let us take the words of Shri Krishna when speaking of the Dharma of the four castes: "Of Brahmanas, Kshattriyas, Vaishyas and Shudras, O Parantapa, the Karmas have been distributed, *according to the gunas born of their own natures*. Serenity, selfrestraint, austerity, purity, forgiveness and also uprightness; wisdom, knowledge, belief in God, are the Brahmana-Karma, born of his own nature. Prowess, splendour, firmness, dexterity, and also not flying from battle, generosity, the nature of a ruler, are the Kshattriya-Karma, born of his own nature. Ploughing, protection of kine, and trade are the Vaishya-Karma, born of his own nature. Action of the nature of service is the Shudra-Karma, born of his own nature. Man reacheth perfection by each being intent on his own Karma".

Then he goes on to say: "Better one's own Dharma, though destitute of merit, than the well executed Dharma of another. He who doeth the Karma laid down by his own nature incurreth not sin".

See how the two words Dharma and Karma are interchanged. They give us the key which we shall use to unlock our problem. Let me give you first a partial definition of Dharma. I cannot make the whole definition clear at once. I will give you the first half of it, dealing with the second half when we come to it. The first half is that "Dharma is the inner nature, which has reached in each man a certain stage of development and unfolding". It is this inner nature which moulds the outer life, which is expressed by thoughts, words, and actions, the inner nature which is born into the environment suited for its further growth. The first idea to grasp is that Dharma is not an outer thing, like the law, or righteousness, or religion, or justice. It is the law of the unfolding life, which moulds all outside it to the expression of itself.

Now in trying to trace out this difficult and abstruse subject, I will treat it under three main divisions. First, Differences, for people have different Dharmas. Even in the passage quoted, four great classes are mentioned. Looking more closely, each individual man has his own Dharma. How shall we understand these? Unless we grasp something of the nature of difference; why they came to be, why they should exist, and what me mean when we speak of differences; unless we understand how each man shows by his thoughts, words, and actions, the stage he has reached; unless we grasp this, we cannot understand Dharma. Then secondly, we shall have to deal with Evolution. For we must trace these differences as they evolve. Lastly, we must deal with the problem of Right and Wrong, for the whole of our study leads up to the answer to the question. "How should a man conduct his life?" It would not be worth while to ask you to follow me, into difficult regions of thought, unless in the end we are to turn our knowledge to good account, and try to lead lives according to Dharma, thus giving to the world that which India was meant to teach.

In what does the perfection of a Universe consist? When we begin to think over a universe and what we mean by it, we find we mean a vast number of separated objects working together more or less harmoniously. Variety is the keynote of the universe, as unity is the note of the Unmanifest, of the Unconditioned - the One without a second. Diversity is the note of the manifested and conditioned - the result of the will to become many.

When a Universe is to come into existence, we learn, the First Cause, the Eternal, the Inconceivable, the Indiscernible, the Subtle, shines forth by His own Will. What that shining forth may mean within Himself none may dare to guess. What it means on the side from which we regard it, that to some extent may be grasped. Ishvara comes forth, but He, coming forth, appears enwrapped in the veil of Maya - there are two sides of the Supreme in manifestation. Many words have been used to express that fundamental pair of opposites: Ishvara and Maya, Sat and Asat, Reality and Unreality, Spirit and Matter, Life and Form. These are words which we, in our limited language, use to express that which is well-nigh beyond the grasp of thinking. All that we can say is: "Thus have the Sages taught us, and thus we in humility repeat".

Ishvara and Maya. What is the universe to he? It is the image of Ishvara reflected in Maya - the perfected image of Ishvara, as He has chosen to condition Himself for this particular universe whose birth-hour is come. His image - limited, conditioned. His Self-conditioned image, the universe is in perfection to declare. But how shall that which is limited, that which is partial, image Ishvara? By the multiplicity of parts working together in one harmonious whole; infinite variety of differences, and the manifold combinations of each with each, shall speak forth the law of the divine thought, until the whole thought is expressed in the totality of that perfected Universe. You should try to catch some glimpse of what this means. Let us together seek to understand.

Ishvara thinks of Beauty; at once His mighty energy, all-potent, generative, strikes upon Maya and develops it into myriad forms of objects that we call beautiful. It touches the matter that is ready to be moulded - for example, water; and the water takes on a million forms of Beauty. We see one in the vast expanse of ocean, still and tranquil, where no wind is blowing, and where the sky is mirrored in its deep bosom. Then we catch another form of Beauty, when the wind lashes it into billows upon billows, and abyss beneath abyss, till the whole mass is terrible in its fury and grandeur. Then a new form of Beauty comes forth from it, and the raging and the foaming waters are hushed, and the ocean is changed into myriad-ripples, glittering and glistening under the moon which shines upon them, her rays broken and bent into a thousand coruscations. And this gives us another hint of what Beauty means. And then we look at the ocean where no land limits the horizon and where the vast expanse is unbroken, and again we stand on the shore and see the waves breaking at our feet. With every change of mood of the sea, its waters speak out a new thought of Beauty. Another glimpse of the thought of Beauty thrown into water we see in the mountain lake, in the stillness and serenity of its quiet bosom; and in the stream that leaps from rock to rock; and in the torrent that dashes itself into millions of spray-drops, catching and refracting the sunlight into all the hues of the rainbow. So from water in every shape and form, from the tossing ocean to the frozen iceberg, from the foggy mists to the gorgeously coloured clouds, bursts forth the thought of Beauty impressed upon it by Ishvara, when the word came forth from Him. When we leave the water, we learn new thoughts of beauty in the tender creeper, in its mass of brilliant colours, in the stronger plant and the sturdier oak, and the dark obscurity of forest depths. New thoughts of Beauty come to us from the face of every mountain peak, and from the vast, rolling prairie where the earth seems to break into new possibilities of life, from the sand of the desert, from the green of the meadow. If we are tired of the earth, the telescope brings to our view the Beauty of myriads of suns, rushing and rolling through the depths of space. Then the microscope reveals to our wondering gaze the Beauty of the infinitely small, as the telescope does of the infinitely great: and thus a new door is opened to us for the contemplation of Beauty. Around us we have thousands and millions of objects that are all beautiful. From the grace of the animal, from the strength of man, from the supple charm of woman, from the dimples of the laughing children, from all these things we catch some glimpses of what the thought of Beauty is in the mind of Ishvara.

In this fashion we may sense something of the way in which His thought broke into myriad forms of splendour, when He spoke as

Beauty to the world. The same is the case with Strength, Energy, Harmony, Music, and so on. You grasp, then, why there should be variety: because no limited thing may fully tell Him, because no limited form may fully express Him. But as each becomes perfect of its kind; all combined may partly reveal Him. Thus the perfection of the Universe is perfection in variety and in the harmony of interrelated parts.

Having reached that conception, we begin to see that the Universe can only gain perfection by each part performing its own function, and developing completely its own share of life. If the tree tries to imitate the mountain, or the water to imitate the earth, each would miss its own beauty and fail to show that of the other. The perfection of the body does not depend upon every cell doing the work of the other cells, but in each cell doing its own part perfectly. We have brain, lungs, heart, digestive organs, and so on. If the brain tried to do the work of the heart, and the lungs tried to digest food, then the body would indeed be in a melancholy condition. The health of the body is secured by each organ doing its own part. We thus realize that as the universe develops, each part is going along the road which is marked out by the law of its own life. The image of Ishvara in nature will never be perfect, until each part is complete in itself and in its relations to the others.

How can these innumerable differences arise? How can all these differences come into existence? How does the Universe, as it evolves as a whole, stand in relation to its parts evolving each on its separate line? We are told that Ishvara, expressing himself on the Prakriti side shows forth three qualities - Sattva, Rajas and Tamas. No English words are equivalent to or can satisfactorily translate these. I may however, for the moment translate Tamas as inertia, the quality that does not move, that gives stability; Rajas is the quality of energy and motion; and Sattva is perhaps best expressed by harmony the quality of pleasure-giving, as all pleasure springs from harmony and only harmony can give it. Then we learn that these three gunas are further modified in seven kinds of ways, seven great lines, as it were, along which innumerable combinations evolve. Every religion speaks of this sevenfold division, every religion proclaims its existence. In Hinduism, they are the five great elements and the two beyond. These are the seven Purushas of whom Manu speaks.

These three gunas combine and divide, arranging themselves into seven great groups, from which arise vast numbers of things by various combinations; remember that into each separate thing each of these qualities enters in different proportions, modified in one of the seven fundamental ways.

From this primary difference brought over from a Universe of the past - for world is linked to world and Universe to Universe - we find that the downpouring life divided and subdivided itself as it fell into matter, till, reaching the circumference of the mighty circle, it rolled back upon itself. Evolution begins at the turning-point, where the wave of life begins to return to Ishvara. The previous stage is the stage of involution, during which this life is becoming involved in matter; in evolution it is unfolding the powers that it contains. We may quote Manu where he says that Ishvara placed His seed in the mighty waters. The life which Ishvara gave was not a developed life, but a life capable of development. Everything exists in germ at first. As the parent gives his life to generate the child, and as that life-seed is built up through many combinations, until it reaches birth, and then year after year, through childhood, youth and manhood, until maturity is reached, and the image of the father is seen again in the son; so does the Eternal Father, when He places the seed in the womb of matter, give the life, but it is not yet evolved. Then it begins its up-climbing, bringing out one phase after another of the life that it is gradually becoming able to express.

As we study the Universe, we find that its varieties differ in their age. This is a thought which bears upon our problem. This world was not brought into its present condition by one creative word. Slowly and gradually and by prolonged meditation did Brahma make the world. One after another living forms came forth. One after another the seeds of life were sown. If you look at any Universe at any point of time, you will find that the variety of that Universe has Time for its chief factor. The age of the developing germ will mark the stage at which that germ has arrived. In a Universe, at one and the same time, there are germs of various ages and stages of development. There are germs younger than minerals, making what are called elemental kingdoms. The developing germs called the mineral kingdom are older than these. Germs evolving as the vegetable world are older than those of the mineral, that is, they have a longer stretch of evolution behind them;

the animals are germs with a yet longer past, and the germs we call humanity have the longest past of all.

Each great class has this diversity as to its beginning in time. So also the separated individual life in one man - not the essential life, but the individual and separated life - is different from that of another, and we differ in the age of our individual existences as we differ in the age of our bodies. The life is one - one life in all; but it is infolded at different stages of time, as regards the starting-point of the seed that there is growing. You should grasp that idea clearly. When a Universe comes to its ending, there will be present in it entities at every stage of growth. I have already said that world is linked to world, and Universe linked to Universe. Some units at the beginning will be at an early stage of evolution; some will be ready to expand ere long into the consciousness of God. In that Universe, when its life-period is over, there will be all the differences of growth dependent upon differences in time. There is one life in all, but the stage of unfoldment of a particular life depends upon the time through which it has been separately evolving. There you grasp the very root of our problem - one life, undying, eternal, infinite as to its source and goal; but that life manifesting itself in different grades of evolution and at different stages of unfoldment, different, amounts of its inherent power showing forth according to the age of the separated life. Those are the two thoughts to grasp, and then you can take the other portion of the definition of Dharma.

Dharma may now be defined as the "inner nature of a thing at any given stage of evolution, and the law of the next stage of its unfolding" - the nature at the point it has reached in unfolding, and then the law which brings about its next stage of unfolding. The nature itself marks out the point in evolution it has reached; then comes what it must do in order to evolve further along its road. Take those two thoughts together, and then you will understand why perfection must be reached by following one's own Dharma. My Dharma is the stage of evolution which my nature has reached in unfolding the seed of divine life which is myself, *plus* the law of life according to which the next stage is to be performed by me. It belongs to this separated self. I must know the stage of my growth, and I must know the law which will enable me to grow further; then I know my Dharma, and by following that Dharma I am going towards perfection.

It is clear then, realizing what this means, why we should each of us study this present condition and this next stage. If we do not know the present stage, we must be ignorant of the next stage which we should aim at, and we may be going against our Dharma and thus delaying our evolution. Or, knowing both, we may work with our Dharma and quicken our evolution. Here comes a great pitfall. We see that a thing is good, noble and great, and we long to accomplish in ourselves that thing. Is it for us the next stage of evolution? Is it the thing which the law of our unfolding life demands, in order that that life may unfold harmoniously? Our immediate aim is not that which is best in itself, but that which is best for us in our present stage, and carries us one step onward. Take a child. There is no doubt that if you take a woman-child, she has before her a future nobler, higher, and more beautiful than the present when she is playing with her dolls; she will be a mother with a baby in her arms instead of a doll; for that is the ideal of perfect womanhood - the mother with the child. But while that is the ideal of a perfect woman, to grasp at that ideal before the time is ripe will do harm and not good. Everything must come in its proper time and place. If that mother is to be developed to the perfection of womanhood, and is to be mother of a family, healthy, strong, able to bear the pressure of the great life-stream, then there must be the period when that child must play with her dolls, must learn lessons, must develop the body. But if, thinking that motherhood is higher and nobler than play, that motherhood should be grasped before its time, and a child be born from a child, the babe suffers, the mother suffers, the nation suffers; and this because the season has not been regarded, the law of unfolding life is violated. All sorts of suffering arise from grasping the fruit ere the fruit is ripe.

I take that example because it is a striking one. It will help you to see why our own Dharma is better for us than the well executed Dharma of another that is not in the line of our unfolding life. That lofty post may be for us in the future, but the time must come, the fruit must ripen. Pluck it ere it is ripe, and your teeth are set on edge. Let it remain on the tree, obeying the law of time and sequential evolution, and the soul will grow according to the power of an endless life.

That then gives us another key to the problem - function is in relation to power. Function grasped before power is developed is mischievous in the extreme to the organism. So we learn the lessons of patience and of waiting on the Good Law. You might judge the progress of a man by his willingness to work with nature and to submit to the law. That is why Dharma is spoken of as law, and sometimes as duty; for both these ideas grow out of the root-thought that it is the inner nature at a given stage of evolution and the law of the next stage of its development. This explains why morality is relative, why duty must differ for every soul, according to the stage of its evolution. When we come to apply this to questions of right and wrong, we shall find that we can solve some of the subtlest problems of morality by dealing with them on this principle. In a conditioned universe, absolute right and wrong are not to be found, but only relative rights and wrongs. The absolute is in Ishvara alone, where it will for ever be found.

Differences are thus necessary for our conditioned consciousness. We think by differences, we feel by differences, and we know by differences. It is only by differences that we know that we are living and thinking men. Unity makes on consciousness no impression. Differences and diversities - those are the things which make the growth of consciousness possible. The unconditioned consciousness is beyond our thinking. We can only think within the limits of the separated and the conditioned.

We can now see how differences in nature come to be, how the time factor comes in, and how, though all have the same nature and will reach the same goal, yet there are differences in the stages of manifestation, and therefore in the laws appropriate for every stage. That is what we need to grasp tonight, before we deal with the complex problem, how this inner nature develops. Truly difficult is the subject, yet the mysteries of the path of action may be cleared for us as we grasp the underlying law, as we recognise the principle of the unfolding life.

May He, who gave Dharma to India as her keynote, illuminate with His unfolding and immortal life, with His light effulgent and unchangeable, these dark minds of ours that dimly try to grasp His law; for only as His blessing falls upon the suppliant seeker, will His law be understood by the mind, will His law be engraven in the heart.

II. EVOLUTION

WE shall deal this evening with the second section of the subject commenced yesterday. You may remember I divided the subject under three heads, for the sake of convenience - Differences, Evolution, and the problem of Right and Wrong. Yesterday we studied the question of Differences - how it came to pass that different men had different Dharmas. I will venture to remind you of the definition of Dharma we adopted; that it means the inner nature, marked by the stage of evolution, *plus* the law of growth for the next stage of evolution. I will ask you to keep that definition in your minds, for without it you will not be able to apply Dharma to what we are to study under the third division of the subject.

Under the head "Evolution", we are to study the way in which the germ of life evolves to the perfect image of God, remembering that we found that that image of God could only be represented by the totality of the numerous objects making up the universe in their details, and that the perfection of the individual depended on the completeness with which he fulfilled his own part in the stupendous whole.

Before we can understand evolution, we must find its spring and motive - a life which involves itself in matter, before it evolves complicated organisms of every kind. We start with the principle that all is from and in God. Nothing in the universe is to be excluded from Him. No life save His life, no force save His force, no energy save His energy, no forms save His forms - all are the results of His thought. That is our fundamental position. That is the ground on which we must stand, daring to accept everything that it implies, daring to recognise everything that it connotes. "The seed of all beings," says Shri Krishna, speaking as the supreme Ishvara, "that am I, O Arjuna! nor is there aught, moving or unmoving, that may exist bereft of Me" (*Bhagavad-Gita, x.* 39.). Do not let us fear to take that central position. Do not, because of the imperfection of the evolving lives, let us shrink from any conclusion to which this truth may lead us.

In another shloka He said: "I am the gambling of the cheat, and the splendour of splendid things I" (x. 36.). What is the meaning of these words that sound so strange? What is the explanation of this phrase which appears almost as profanity? Not only in this discourse do we find this position enunciated, but we find that Manu teaches exactly the same truth: "From Himself He produces the universe". The life coming forth from the Supreme puts on veil after veil of Maya, in which that life is to evolve all the perfections that lie latent within it.

Now the first question is: Does not this life, which comes from Ishvara, already contain within itself everything already developed, every manifested power, every possibility realized as actuality? The answer to that question, spoken over and over again, in symbols, allegories, and distinct words, is "No". It contains everything in potency, but nothing at first in manifestation. It contains everything in germ, but nothing at first as developed organism. The seed is that which is placed in the mighty waters of matter, the germ alone is given forth by the Life of the World. Those germs, which come from the life of Ishvara, evolve - step by step, stage after stage, on one rung of a ladder after another - all the powers that reside in the generating Father, the name that Ishvara gives to Himself in the *Gita*. He declares once more: "My womb is the Mahat-Brahma; in that I place the germ; thence cometh the production of all beings, O Bharata. In whatsoever wombs mortals are produced, O Kaunteya, the Mahat-Brahma is their womb, I their generating Father" (xiv. 3-4.). From that seed - from that germ containing everything in possibility but nothing as yet in manifestation - from that seed is to evolve a life, stage by stage, rising higher and higher, until at last a centre of consciousness is formed capable of expanding to the consciousness of Ishvara, while remaining as a centre still, with the power to come forth as a new Logos, or Ishvara, for the production of a new universe.

Let us take this vast sweep of thought in detail. Life involved in matter - that is our beginning. These germs of life, these myriad seeds, or to use the Upanishadic phrase, these numberless sparks, all come forth from the one Flame which is the supreme Brahman. Qualities are now to be brought out of these seeds. Those qualities are powers, but powers manifested through matter. One by one those powers will be brought out - powers which are the life of Ishvara as veiled in Maya. Slow is the growth in the early stages, hidden as the seed underground is hidden, when first it strikes its root downward, and sends its tender offshoot upward in order that later on the growing tree may appear. In silence germinates this divine seed, and the early beginnings are hidden in darkness, like the roots under the ground.

This power in the life, or rather these innumerable powers which Ishvara manifests in order that the universe may be, these myriad powers are at first unapparent in the germ – no sign of the mighty possibilities, no trace of what it is hereafter to become. A word is spoken as to this manifestation in matter, which throws much light on the subject, if we can grasp its inner and subtler meaning. Shri Krishna, speaking of His lower Prakriti, or inferior manifestation, says: "Earth, water, fire, air, ether, Manas and Buddhi also and Ahamkara - these are the eightfold divisions of My Prakriti. This the inferior". Then He says what is His higher Prakriti: "Know My other Prakriti, the higher, the life-element, O mightyarmed, by which the universe is upheld" (vii. 4, 5.). Then a little later, separated by many shlokas, so that sometimes the connecting link is missed, other words are spoken: "This divine Maya of Mine, guna-made, is hard to pierce; they who come to Me they cross over this Maya" (vii. 14.). This Yoga-Maya is, truly, hard to pierce; many do not discover Him involved in Maya, so hard to pierce it is, so difficult to discover. "Those without Buddhi think of Me, the unmanifest, as having manifestation; knowing not My supreme nature, imperishable, most excellent. Nor am I of all discovered, enveloped in My Yoga-Maya" (vii. 24, 25.). Then He further declares that by His unmanifested life it is that the universe is pervaded. The life-element, or higher Prakriti, is unmanifested, the lower Prakriti is manifested. Then He says: "From the unmanifested all the manifested stream forth at the coming of day; at the coming of night they dissolve, even in That called the unmanifested" (viii: 18.). This occurs over and over again. Then further on He declares: "Therefore verily there existeth, higher than that unmanifested, another unmanifested, eternal, which, in the destroying of all beings, is not destroyed" (viii. 20.). There is a subtle distinction between Ishvara and the image of Himself which He sends forth. The image is the reflected unmanifest, but Himself is the higher unmanifest, the eternal that never is destroyed.

Realizing that, we come to the drawing out of powers. Here we begin really our evolution. The outpouring life was involved in matter, in order to bring the seed into the matter-surrounded conditions which should make evolution possible. When we come to the first germinating of the seed, our difficulty comes in. For we must throw ourselves, in thought, to the time when there was no reason in this embryonic self, no imaginative faculty, no memory, no judgment, none of the conditioned faculties of the mind that we know of; when all the life that was manifested was that which we find in the mineral kingdom, with the lowest conditions of consciousness. The minerals manifest consciousness by their attractions and repulsions, by their holding together of particles, by their affinities for each other, by their repellings of each other, but they show none of that consciousness that can be called the recognition of the "I" and the "not-I".

In every one of these lowest forms in the mineral kingdom, Ishvara's life is beginning to unfold. Not only is the germ of life there evolving, but He, in all His might and power, is there in every atom of His universe. His the moving life which makes evolution inevitable. His the force expanding gently the walls of matter, with immense patience and watching love, in order that they may not break under the strain. God, Himself the Father of the life, holds that life within Himself as Mother, unfolding the seed unto the likeness of Himself, never impatient, never hurrying, willing to give as much time from the countless ages as the little germ may require. Time is nothing to Ishvara, for He is eternal and to Him all Is. It is the perfection of manifestation that He seeks, and there is no hurrying in His work. And we shall see, later on, how this infinite patience works out. The man, who is to be the image of his Father, shows within him the reflection of the Self with which he is one, and whence he came.

The life is to be awakened, but how? By blows, by vibrations, the inner essence is called into activity. Life is stirred to activity by vibrations that touch it from outside. These myriad seeds of life, not yet conscious of themselves, matter-enveloped, are thrown against each other in the myriad processes of nature; but "nature" is only the garment of God, is only the lowest manifestation in which He shows Himself on the material plane. These forms strike against each other, shaking thus the outer shells of matter in which the life is involved, and the life within gives a quiver as the blow is delivered.

Now the nature of the blow is of no importance. All that is important is that the blow shall be strong. Any experience is useful. Anything which strikes that shell so forcibly that the life within quivers in response is all that is wanted at first. The life within must be made to quiver. That will awaken some dawning power in the life. At first it is only a quiver within itself, and nothing more than a quiver, with no result on its outer shell. But as blow after blow is repeated, and vibration after vibration sends in its earthquake shocks, the life within sends out, through its own enveloping shell, a thrill of answer. The blow has provoked an answer. Another stage is thus touched - the answer comes forth from the hidden life and goes out beyond the shell. This goes on through the mineral kingdom and the vegetable kingdom. In the vegetable kingdom the answers to the vibrations caused by contact begin to show a new power of the life - sensation. The life begins to show out in itself what we call "feeling"; that is, different answers are given to pleasure and to pain. Pleasure is fundamentally harmonious. All that gives pleasure is harmonious. All that gives pain is discordant. Think of music. Rhythmical notes, struck together as a chord, give to the ear a sensation of pleasure. But if you strike your finger on the strings without paying attention to the notes, you make a discord, which gives pain to the ear. That which is true of music is true everywhere. Health is harmony, disease is discord. Strength is harmony, weakness is discord. Beauty is harmony, ugliness is discord. All through nature pleasure means the answer of a sentient being to vibrations that are harmonious and rhythmical, and pain means its answer to those that are discordant and unrhythmical. The rhythmical vibrations make an outward channel through which the life can expand, and this pouring forth is "pleasure"; the unrhythmical close up the channels and frustrate the forth-pouring, and this frustration is "pain".* [* The student should work out in detail this fundamental principle; he will thereby much clarify his thoughts.] The forth-pouring of life towards objects is what we name "desire"; hence pleasure becomes the gratification of desire. This difference begins to make itself felt in the vegetable kingdom. A blow comes that is harmonious. The life answers to that in harmonious vibrations and expands, feeling in that expansion "pleasure". A blow comes that is a jangle. Life answers to that discordantly, is checked, and feels in that check "pain". The blows are given over and over again, and not until the repetition has occurred a myriad times does a recognition of the distinction between the two begin to arise in that imprisoned life. Only by making distinctions is our consciousness, as at present constituted, able to distinguish objects from each other. Take a very common illustration. Let a piece of money lie in the palm of the hand and close your fingers round it; you feel it; but as the pressure is continued, without any variation, the sensation of feeling in the hand disappears and you do not know that your hand is not empty. Move a finger and you feel the money; keep the hand still, and the sensation vanishes. Thus consciousness can only know things by differences. And when difference is eliminated, consciousness ceases to respond.

We come to the next thing which is manifested as the life evolves through the animal kingdom. Pleasure and pain are now acutely felt, and a germ of recognition, connecting objects and sensations, begins; we call it "perception". What does this mean? It means that the life develops the power of forming a link between the object that impresses it and the sensation by which it responds to the object. When that dawning life, contacting an external object, knows it as an object that gives pleasure or pain, then we say that the object is perceived, and the faculty of perception, or the making of links between the outer and the inner worlds, is evolved when that is established; mental power begins to germinate and to grow within that organism; we find it in the higher animals.

Let us take it in the savage man, where we shall be able to pass more rapidly over these early stages. We find the consciousness of "I" and "not-I" slowly establishing itself in him - the two going together. "Not-I" touches him, and "I" feels it; "not-I" gives him pleasure, and "I" knows it; "not-I" gives him pain, and "I" suffers it. A distinction is now being made between the feeling, thought of as "I", and all that causes it, thought of as "not-I". Here commences intelligence, and the root of self-consciousness is beginning to develop. That is, *a centre* is being formed, to which everything goes in and from which everything comes out.

I spoke of repetition of vibrations, and now repetition produces results more rapidly. As repetition causes the perception of pleasure-giving objects, the next stage is developed, the expectation of pleasure before the contact takes place. The object is recognised as one that has given pleasure on previous occasions; a repetition of the pleasure is expected, and that expectation is the dawn of memory and the beginning of imagination, the interweaving of intellect with desire. Because the object has given pleasure before, it is expected to give pleasure again. Thus expectation brings into manifestation another germinating quality of the mind. When we have the recognition of the object and the expectation of pleasure from its return, the next stage is the making and vivifying of a mental image of that object – the memory of it - thus causing an outflow of desire, desire to have that object, a longing for that object, and finally a going forth in search of that object that gives pleasurable sensation. Thus the man becomes full of active desires. He desires pleasure, and is moved to seek it by the mind. For a long time he had remained in the animal stage, when he would never seek for a thing unless the actual sensation in his inner body made him want something that the outer world alone could satisfy. Just for one moment return to the animal; think what stirs the animal to action. A craving to get rid of an unpleasant sensation. He feels hunger, he desires food, and he goes in search of it; he feels thirst, he desires to quench it, and he goes in search of water. Thus he always goes in search of the object that will gratify the desire. Give him the gratification of desire and he is quiet. There is no self-initiated motion in the animal. The push must come from outside. True, the hunger is in the inner body, but that is outside the centre of consciousness. The evolution of consciousness may be traced by the proportion which the outside stimulus to action bears to the self-initiated stimulus. The lower consciousness is stimulated to activity by impulses coming from outside itself. The higher consciousness is stimulated to activity by motion initiated within.

Now as we deal with our savage man, we find that the gratification of desire is the law of his progress. How strange that sounds to many of you. Says Manu: Seeking to get rid of desires by gratifying them is like trying to quench the fire by pouring butter over it. Desire must be curbed and restrained. Desire is to be extinguished utterly. This is most certainly true, but only when a man has reached a certain stage of evolution. In the early stages, the gratification of desires is the law of evolution. If he does not gratify his desires, no growth for him is possible. You must realise that at that stage there is nothing which can be called morality. There is no distinction between right and wrong. Every desire should be gratified; when this commencing centre of self-consciousness is seeking to gratify desires, then alone it grows. In this lowest stage the Dharma of the savage man, or of the higher animal, is imposed on him. He does not choose; his inner nature, marked by the development of desire, demands gratification. The law of his growth is the satisfaction of these desires. So that the Dharma of the savage is the gratification of every desire. And you find in him no consciousness of right or wrong, not the faintest dawning notion that the gratification of desires is forbidden by some higher law.

Without that gratification of desires there is no further growth. All that growth must precede the dawning of reason and judgment and the development of the higher powers of memory and imagination. All these things must be evolved by the gratification of desire. Experience is the law of life, it is the law of growth. Unless he gathers experiences of every kind, he cannot know that he lives in a world of Law. Two ways does the law find for impressing itself on man: pleasure when the Law is followed, pain when the Law is opposed. If men did not at that early stage have every sort of experience, how could they learn of the existence of the Law? How can discrimination grow between right and wrong, unless there is the experience of both good and evil? A universe can never come into existence except by the pairs of opposites, and these at one stage appear in the consciousness as good and evil. You cannot know light without darkness, motion without rest, pleasure without pain; so you cannot know the good that is harmony with the Law with out knowing the evil that is discord with the Law. Good and evil are a pair of opposites in the later evolution of man, and man cannot become conscious of the difference between them unless he has experience of both.

Now we come to a change. Man has developed a certain power of discrimination. Left to himself utterly, he would come to know in time that some things help him on, that some things strengthen him, that some things increase his life; also that other things weaken him and diminish his life. Experience would teach him all that. Left only to the teaching of experience he would come to know right from wrong, would identify the pleasure-giving that increased life with the right, and the pain-giving that diminished life with the wrong, and would thus reach the conclusion that all happiness and growth lay in obeying the Law. But it would take a very long time for this dawning intelligence to compare together experiences of pleasure and pain, and the confusing experiences in which that which at first gave pleasure became painful by excess, and then to deduce from them the principle of law. It would be a very long time before he could put innumerable experiences together, and deduce from them the idea that this thing is right, and that thing is wrong. But he is not left unaided to make that deduction. There come to him, from past worlds, Intelligences more highly evolved than his own, Teachers who come to help on his evolution, to train his growth, to tell him of the existence of a law determining that which will bring about his more rapid evolution, increasing his happiness, intelligence and strength. In fact, revelation from the mouth of a Teacher quickens evolution, and instead of man being left to the slow teaching of experience, the expression of the law from the mouth of a superior is made to assist his growth.

The Teacher comes and says to this dawning intelligence: "If you kill that man, you are doing an action that I forbid on divine authority. That action is *wrong*. It will bring misery". The Teacher says: "It is *right* to help the starving; that starving man is your brother; feed him; do not let him starve; share with him what you have. That action is *right*, and if you obey that law it will be well with you". Rewards of actions are held out to attract the dawning intelligence towards good, and punishments and threats to warn him from wrong. Earthly prosperity is joined with obedience of law, earthly misery with disobedience to law. This announcement of the law that misery follows on that which the law forbids, and happiness on that which the law commands, stimulates the dawning intelligence. He disregards the law, the penalty follows, and he suffers; and he says: "The Teacher told me so". Memory of a command proved by experience makes an impression on the consciousness far more quickly and more strongly than does experience alone without the revealed law. By this declaration of what the learned call the fundamental principles of morality, namely, that certain classes of actions retard evolution and other classes of action quicken evolution - by this declaration intelligence is immensely stimulated.

If a man will not obey the law declared, then he is left to the hard teaching of experience. If he says: "I will have that thing, though the law forbid it," then he is left to the stern teaching of pain, and the whip of suffering teaches the lesson that he would not learn from the lips of love.

How often that happens now. How often a young man, argumentative and self-conceited, will not listen to law, will not listen to the experienced, pays no regard to the training of the past. Desire conquers intelligence. His father is heart-broken. "My son is plunged into vice," says he; "my son is going into evil. I instructed him in right conduct, and see, he has become a liar; my heart is broken for my son."

But Ishvara, the Father more loving than any earthly father, has patience. For he is in the son as much as in the father. He is in him teaching him a lesson, in the only way by which that soul is willing to learn. He would not learn by authority or by example. At all hazards that desire for the evil thing which is stopping his evolution must be rooted out of his nature. If he will not learn by gentleness, let him then learn by pain. Let him learn by experience; let him plunge into vice, and reap the bitter pang that comes from trampling on the law. There is time; he will learn the lesson surely though painfully. God is in him, and still He lets him go that way; nay, He even opens the way that he may go along it; when he demands it, the answer of God is: "My child, if you will not listen, take your own way and learn your lesson in the fire of your agony and in the bitterness of your degradation. I am with you still, watching over you and your actions, the Fulfiller of the law and the Father of your life. You shall learn in the mire of degradation that cessation of desire which you would not learn from wisdom and from love". That is why He says in the *Gita*: "I am the gambling of the cheat". For He is always patiently working for the glorious end, by rough ways if we will not walk in smooth. We, unable to understand that infinite compassion, misread Him, but He works on with the patience of eternity, in order that desire may be utterly uprooted, and His son may be perfect as his Father in heaven is perfect.

Let us go on the next stage. There are certain great laws of growth that are general. We have learned to look upon certain things as right and upon others as wrong. Every nation has its own standard of morality. Only a few know how that standard was formed, and where that standard fails. For ordinary affairs the standard is good enough. The experience of the race has found out, under the guidance of law, that some actions hold back evolution while others press it forward. The great law of the orderly evolution that follows the earlier stages is the law of the four successive steps in later human growth. This comes after a man has reached a certain point, after the preliminary training is over. It is found in every nation at a certain stage of evolution, but was proclaimed in ancient India as the definite law of evolving life, as the sequential order of the growth of soul, as the underlying principle by which Dharma may be understood and followed. Dharma, remember, includes two things - the inner nature at the point it has reached, and the law of its growth for the next stage. For every man

Dharma is to be declared. The first Dharma is that of *service*. No matter in what land the souls may be born, when they have passed through the earlier stages, then their inner nature demands the discipline of service, and that they should learn by service the qualities that are needed for growth into the next stage. At this stage the power of independent action is very limited. At this comparatively early stage, there is more tendency to yield to impulse from without, than to show a developed judgment, choosing a particular course from within. In this class are seen all those who belong to the serving type. Remember those wise words of Bhishma, that if the characteristics of a Brahmana are found in a Shudra and are not found in a Brahmana, then that Brahamana is not a Brahmana and that Shudra is not a Shudra. In other words, the characteristics of the inner nature mark out the stage of that soul's growth, and stamp it as belonging to one great natural division or another. When the power of initiation is small, where the judgment is untrained, where the reason is poor and little developed, where the Self is unconscious of his high destiny, where he is chiefly moved by desire, where he is still to grow by the gratification of most but not all desires, that man is one whose Dharma is service, and only by performing that Dharma can he follow the law of growth by which he will reach perfection. And such a man is Shudra, by whatever name he may be called in different countries. In ancient India, the souls bearing the characteristics of this type were born into the classes that suited them, for Devas guided their births. In this age, however, confusion has supervened.

What is the law of growth in that stage? Obedience, devotion, fidelity. That is the law of growth for that stage. Obedience, because the judgment is not developed. He whose Dharma is service has to blindly obey the one to whom he renders service. His is not to challenge the order of his superior, nor his to see that the commanded action is a wise one. He has received an order to do a thing, and his Dharma is obedience, by which alone he will be able to learn. People hesitate at that teaching, but it is true. I will take an example, that will strike you most forcibly - that of an army, of a private soldier under the command of his Captain. If every private soldier were to use his own judgment as to the orders that came from the General, and if he were to say: "This is not well, for in my judgment that is the place where I shall be more serviceable", what would become of the army? The private soldier is shot if he disobeys, for his duty is obedience. When your judgment is feeble, when you are chiefly moved by impulses from without, when you cannot be happy without noise and clatter and jangle around you, then your Dharma is service, wherever you may be born, and you are happy if your karma leads you to a position where discipline will train you.

So the man learns to prepare for the next stage. And the duty of all those who are in positions of authority is to remember that the Dharma of a Shudra is fulfilled when he is obedient and faithful to his master, and they should not expect one in that grade of evolution to show forth the higher virtues. To demand from him cheerfulness in suffering, purity of thought, and the power to suffer hardships ungrudgingly, is to demand too much; for when we ourselves often do not show these qualities, how can we expect them from those whom we call the lower classes? The duty of the higher is to show forth the higher virtues, but he has no right to demand them from his inferiors. If the servant shows fidelity and obedience, the Dharma is perfectly performed, and other faults should not be punished, but should be gently pointed out by the master, for by so doing he is training that younger soul; for a child soul should be gently led along the path, and its growth should not be stunted by harsh treatment, as we generally stunt it.

Then the soul, having learned this lesson in many births, by learning the lesson has obeyed the law of growth, and by following his Dharma has approached the next stage, in which he is to learn the first use of power by acquiring wealth. Then the Dharma of that soul is to evolve all the qualities which are now ready for evolution, and are brought out by leading the life which the inner nature demands, i.e. by taking up some occupation which the next stage requires, the stage where it is a merit to acquire wealth. For the Dharma of a Vaishya all over the world is to evolve certain definite faculties. The faculty of justice, just dealing between man and man, the not swerving aside at the mere prompting of sentiment, the working out of the qualities of shrewdness, keenness, and holding a just balance between contending duties, fair payment in fair exchange, acuteness of insight, frugality, absence of waste and extravagance, the exaction from every servant of the service that should be given, the payment of just wages, but only of just wages - these are the characteristics which fit him for higher growth. It is a merit in the Vaishya to be frugal, to refuse to pay more than he should, to insist on a just and fair exchange. All these things bring out qualities that are wanted and will conduce to future perfection. In their early stages they are sometimes unlovely, but from the higher standpoint they are the Dharma of that man, and if it be not fulfilled, there will be weakness in the character, which will come out later and injure his evolution. Liberality is indeed the law of his further growth, but not the liberality of carelessness or of over-payment. He is to gather wealth by the exercise of frugality and strictness, and then to spend that wealth on noble objects and on learned men, to bestow it upon worthy and well considered schemes for the public good. To gather with energy and shrewdness, and to spend with careful discrimination and liberality, that is the Dharma of a Vaishya, the outcome of his nature and the law of his further growth.

This leads us to the next stage, that of the rulers and warriors, of battles and struggles, where the inner nature is combative, aggressive, quarrelsome, standing on its own ground and ready to protect every one in the enjoyment of what is right. Courage, fearlessness, splendid generosity, throwing away of life in the defense of the weak and in the discharging of one's duties - that is the Dharma of the Kshattriya. His duty is to protect what is given him in charge against all aggression from without. It may cost him life but never mind that. He must do his duty. To protect, to guard, that is his work. His strength is to be a barrier between the weak and the oppressive, between the helpless and those who would trample them under foot. Right for him the following of war and the struggle in the jungle with the wild beast. Because you do not understand what evolution is, and what the law of growth, you stand aghast at the horrors of war. But the great Rishis, who made this order, knew that a weak soul can never attain perfection. You cannot get strength without courage, and firmness and courage cannot be got without the facing of danger, and the readiness to throw away life when duty demands the sacrifice.

Our sentimental, weak-kneed, pseudo-moralist shrinks from that teaching. But he forgets that in every nation there are souls that need that training, and whose further evolution depends upon their success in attaining it. I appeal again to Bhishma, the incarnation of Dharma, and I remember what he said, that it is the duty of the Kshattriya to slay thousands of his enemies, if his duty in protection lies in that direction. War is terrible, fighting is shocking, our hearts revolt from it, and we shrink before the anguish of mutilated and mangled bodies. To a great extent this is because we are utterly deluded by form. The one use of the body is to enable the life within it to evolve. But the moment it has learned all that that body can give it, let the body break away, and let the soul go free to take a new body that will enable it to manifest higher powers. We cannot pierce the Maya of the Lord. These bodies of ours may perish, time after time, but every death is a resurrection to higher life. This body itself is nothing more than a garment which the soul puts on, and no wise men would like the body to be eternal. We clothe our child in a small coat and change it when the child grows. But will you make the coat of iron, and cramp the growth of the child? So this body is our coat. Shall it be then of iron that it should never perish? Does not the soul require a new body for its higher growth? Let then the body go. This is the hard lesson the Kshattriya learns, and so he throws away his bodily life, and, in this throwing away, his soul gains the power of self-sacrifice, he learns endurance, fortitude, courage, resource, devotion to an ideal, loyalty to a cause, and he pays his body gladly as the price for these, the immortal soul rising triumphant and preparing for a nobler life.

Then there comes the last stage, the stage of teaching. The Dharma of that stage is to teach. The soul must have assimilated all lower experiences before he can teach. If he had not been through all those previous stages, and obtained wisdom through obedience and exertion and combat, how could he be a teacher? He has reached the stage of evolution where the natural expansion of his inner nature is to teach his more ignorant brethren. These qualities are not artificial. They are inborn qualities of nature and they show themselves wherever they exist. A Brahmana is not a Brahmana if he is not a teacher by his Dharma. He has gained knowledge and a favourable birth in order to make him a teacher.

The law of his growth is knowledge, piety, forgiveness, being the friend of every creature. How the Dharma is changed! But he could not be the friend of every creature if he had not learned to throw his life away when duty called, and the very battle trained the Kshattriya to become at a later stage the friend of every creature. What is the law of a Brahmanas growth? He must never take offence. He must never lose self-control. He must never be hasty. He must always be gentle: otherwise he falls from his Dharma. He must be all purity. He must never lead an evil life. He must detach himself from worldly things, if they have a hold upon him. Do I hold up an impossible standard? I but speak the law as the Great Ones have spoken it, and I but feebly re-echo their words. The law has laid down the standard, and who shall dare to lower it? When Shri Krishna Himself proclaimed that as the Dharma of the Brahmana, that must be the law of his growth, and the end of his growth is liberation. For him is liberation, but only if he shows out the qualities that he ought to have reached, and follows the lofty ideal that is his Dharma. These are the only justification for the name of Brahmana.

This ideal is so beautiful that all earnest and thoughtful men desire to reach it. But wisdom steps in and says: "Yes, it shall be yours, but you must earn it. You must grow, you must labour; truly it is yours, but it is not yours until you have paid the price". Important is it for our own growth, and the growth of the nations, that this distinction in Dharmas should be understood as depending upon the stage of evolution, and that we should be able to discriminate our own Dharma by the characteristics which we find in our nature. If we set before an unprepared soul an ideal so lofty that it does not move him, we check his evolution. If you give to a peasant the ideal of a Brahmana you are placing before him an impossible ideal, and the result is that he does nothing. When you tell a man a thing too high for him, that man knows that you have been talking nonsense, for you have commanded him to perform that which he has no power to perform; your folly has placed before him motives which do not move him. But wise were the teachers of old. They gave the children sugar-plums, and later the higher lessons. But we are so clever that we appeal to the lowest sinner by motives which can stir only the highest saint, and thus instead of furthering, we check his evolution. Place your own ideal as high as you can set it. But do not impose your ideal upon your brother, the law of whose growth may be entirely different from yours. Learn the tolerance which helps each man to do in his place what it is good for him to do, and what his nature impels him to do. Leaving him in his place, help him. Learn that tolerance which is repelled by none, however sinful, which sees in every man a divinity working, and stands beside him to help him. Instead of standing off on some high peak of spirituality, and preaching a doctrine of self-sacrifice which is utterly beyond his comprehension, in teaching his young soul, use his higher selfishness to destroy the lower. Do not tell the peasant that when he is not industrious he is falling from the ideal; but tell that man: "There is your wife; you love that woman; she is starving. Set to work and feed her". By that motive, which is certainly selfish, you do more to raise that man than if you preach to him about Brahman, the unconditioned and unmanifest. Learn what Dharma means, and you will be of service to the world.

I do not wish to lower by one tiniest fraction your own ideal; you cannot aim too high. The fact that you can conceive it makes it yours, but does not make it that of your less developed younger brother. Aim at the loftiest you are able to think and to love. But in aiming, consider the means as well as the end, your powers as well as your aspirations. Make your aspirations high. They are the germs of powers in your next life. Through ever keeping the ideal high you will grow towards it, and what you long for today you shall be in the days to come. But have the tolerance of knowledge, and the patience which is divine. Each thing in its own place is in its right place. As the higher nature develops you can appeal to the qualities of self-sacrifice, purity and utter self-devotion, to the will firmly fixed on God. That is the ideal for the highest to accomplish. Let us climb towards it gradually, lest we fail to reach it at all.

III. RIGHT AND WRONG

DURING the last two days of our study, we have been giving our attention and fixing our thought on what I may call the theoretical side, to a very great extent, of this complicated and difficult problem. We have tried to understand how the differences of nature arise. We have tried to grasp the sublime idea, that this world is intended to grow from the mere germ of life given out by God into the image of Him who gave it forth. The perfection of that image, we have seen, can only be gained by the multiplicity of finite objects, and perfection lies in that multiplicity; but in that same multiplicity we see is implied necessarily the limitation of each object. We then found that by the law of growth, we must have existing in the universe, at one and the same time, every variety of inner evolving nature. As these natures are all at different stages of evolution, we cannot make on all of them the same demands, nor expect from all of them the discharge of the same functions.

Morality must be studied in relation to the people who are to practice it. In judging the standard of right and wrong for a particular individual, we must consider at what stage of growth that individual has arrived. Absolute right existeth in Ishvara alone; our right and wrong are relative and depend for each of us very much on the stage of evolution that we have reached.

I am going to try this evening to apply this theory to the conduct of life. We must see whether we have gained, by the line of study that we have pursued, a rational and scientific idea of morality, so that we may no longer have the same confusion that is seen today. For we see that ideals are held up on one side as those which ought to be reproduced in life, and on the other hand we find that there is an absolute failure even to aim at these ideals; we behold a most unfortunate divergence between faith and practice. Morality is not without its laws; like everything else in a universe that is the expression of divine thought, morality has also its conditions and limitations. In this way it may be possible to bring a cosmos out of the present moral chaos, and to learn practical lessons in morality, which will enable India to grow, to develop, to become again an example to the world, reproducing her ancient grandeur, showing forth once more her ancient spirituality.

There are three recognised schools of morality existing among western people. We must remember that western thought is very largely influencing India, and especially is it influencing the rising generation, on which the hope of India rests. It is, therefore, necessary that we should understand something of these schools of morality, differing in their theories and teachings, that exist in the West, if it be only in order to learn to avoid their limitations, and to take from them whatever of good they may have to offer.

There is one school which says that revelation from God is the basis of morality. The objection raised by opponents to that statement is that in this world there are many religions, and every religion has its own revelation. Looking at this variety of religious scriptures, it is argued, it is difficult to say that one revelation is to be regarded as based on supreme authority. That each religion will regard its own revelation as supreme is natural, but in this conflict of tongues how shall a decision be made by the student?

Then it is said again, that there is an inherent defect in this theory, affecting all moral standards founded on a revelation given once for all.

In order that a scheme may be useful for the time for which it is given, it must be of a nature suitable for the time. As a nation evolves, and thousands upon thousands of years pass over the people, we find that that which was suitable for the nation in its infancy, becomes unsuitable for the nation in its manhood; many precepts once useful are no longer useful today under the changed circumstances of the time. That difficulty is recognised and met when we come to deal with the Hindu scriptures; for we find there a vast variety of moral teachings, suitable for all grades of evolving souls. There are precepts so simple, so clear, so definite, and so imperative, that the youngest of souls may utilize them. But we find also that the Rishis recognised that these precepts were not meant for the training of a highly developed soul. We find in the Ancient Wisdom that teachings were also given to a few advanced souls, teachings that at the time were utterly unintelligible to the masses. Those teachings were restricted to an inner circle of those who had reached the maturity of the human race. Different schools of morality have always been recognised in Hinduism as necessary for human growth. But whenever, in some great religion, that recognition is not found, you get a certain theoretical morality, not suited to the growing needs of the people, and, therefore, there is a sense of unreality, a feeling that it is not reasonable to permit now what was permitted in the infancy of humanity. On the other hand, you find here and there, in all scriptures, precepts of the loftiest character which few can even strive to obey. When a command, suitable to the almost savage, is made of universal obligation and is given on the same authority and to the same people as the command given to the saint, there creeps in the feeling of unreality, and confusion of thought is the result.

Another school has arisen, which bases morality on intuition - which says that God speaks to every man through the voice of conscience. It alleges that revelation is made to nation after nation, but that we are not bound by any single book; conscience is the final arbiter. The objection made to this theory is that one man's conscience has the same authority as another man's. If your conscience differs from that of another, then who may decide between conscience and conscience, between the conscience of the ignorant rustic and the conscience of the illuminated mystic? If you say that you admit the principle of evolution, and that you should take as your judge the highest conscience in the race, then intuition fails as a solid basis of morality, and the very element of variety destroys the rock on which you intended to build. The conscience is the voice of the inner man, who remembers the experiences of his past, and out of that immemorial experience judges a given line of conduct today. This so-called intuition is the result of countless incarnations, and according to the number of incarnations, the mind is evolved on which the quality of the conscience of the present individual depends; such intuition, pure and simple, cannot be taken as sufficient guide in morality. We want a commanding voice, not a jangle of tongues. We need the authority of the teacher, and not the confused gabbling of the crowd.

The third school of morality is the school of utilitarianism. That school's view is, as generally presented, neither reasonable nor satisfactory. What is the maxim of this school?"That is right which conduces to the greatest happiness of the greatest number." It is a maxim which will not bear analysis. Notice the words "greatest number". Such a limitation makes the maxim one which the illuminated intelligence must reject. There is no question of majority, when we are dealing with mankind. One life is its root, one God its goal; you cannot separate the happiness of one from that of another. You cannot break up the solid unity, and, picking up the majority, give happiness to them, and leave the minority disregarded. This theory does not recognise the irrefragable unity of the human race, and consequently its maxim fails as a basis of morality. It fails because, in consequence of this unity, one man cannot be perfectly happy unless all men are perfectly happy. His happiness fails in perfection so long as one unit is left out and is unhappy. God does not make distinctions as to units and majorities, but gives one life to humanity and to all creatures. The life of God is the only life in the universe; and the perfect happiness of that life is the goal of the universe.

Then again, there is a failure in this maxim as an impelling motive because it appeals only to the developed intelligence, that is, to the highly evolved soul. If you go to the ordinary man of the world, to a selfish person, and if you say to that man: "You must lead a life of self-sacrifice and virtue and perfect morality, even though the leading it may cost you your life," what do you think would be his answer? Such a man would say: "Why should I do this for the human race, for people in the future whom I shall never see?" If you take this as the standard of right and wrong, then the martyr becomes the greatest fool that humanity has ever produced, for he throws away the possibility of happiness and gets nothing in return. You cannot take this standard, save by limiting your view to the cases in which you get a noble soul, highly developed, and, though not entirely spiritual, with possibility of dawning spirituality. There are such as William Kingdom Clifford, in whose hands the utilitarian doctrine has become inspired with a sublime loftiness of tone. Clifford, in his essay on Ethics, appeals to the highest ideals and gives the noblest teachings of self-sacrifice. He had no belief in the immortality of the soul; approaching death, he could stand beside his grave, believing that that ended all, and preach that the highest virtue is the only thing that a true man can practice, since he owes it to a world which has given him all. But very few will draw inspiration so noble from a prospect so gloomy, and we need a view of right and wrong that shall inspire all, appeal to all, and not merely to those who need its impulse least.

What has come out of all this quarrelling? Confusion, and something worse. A lip-acceptance of revelation, with a practical disregard of it. We have, in fact, a revelation modified by custom. That is the standard which emerges from this confusion. Revelation is taken theoretically as authority, but is disregarded in practice, because often found imperfect. So that you have this unreasonable position, that that which is declared as authority is rejected in the life, and a life of an illogical kind, a happy-go-lucky life is led, without any logic or reason, without the basis of any definite and rational system.

Can we find in this idea of Dharma a basis more satisfactory, a basis on which the conduct of life may be intelligently built? However low, or however high the stage of evolution occupied by the individual, the idea of Dharma gives us the thought of an inner nature unfolding itself in further growth, and we have found that the world is, as a whole, evolving - evolving from the imperfect to the perfect, from the germ to the divine man, stage by stage, in every grade of manifested life. That evolution is by the divine will. God is the moving power, the guiding Spirit of the whole. It is His way of building the world. It is the method that He has adopted in order that the Spirits that are His children may reproduce the likeness of their Parent. Does not that very statement hint at a law? That is right, which works with the divine purpose in the evolution of the universe, and forwards that evolution from the imperfect to the perfect. That is wrong, which delays or frustrates that divine purpose, and tends to push the universe back to the stage from which it is evolving. It is growing from the mineral to the vegetable, from the vegetable to the animal, from the animal to the animal-man, and from the animal-man to the divine man. That is right, which helps the evolution towards divinity; that is wrong, which drags it backwards, or impedes its progress.

Now if we look for a moment at that idea, perhaps we shall acquire a clear view of this law, and no longer feel uneasy over this relative aspect of right and wrong. Place a ladder with its foot on the platform and let it rise to some place beyond the roof. Suppose that one of you had climbed five steps up, another two steps, while a third was standing on the platform. For the man who had climbed up five steps to stand beside the man who was on the second step would be to descend; but for the man on the platform to stand beside the man on the second step would to be ascend. Suppose that every rung of the ladder represents an action: each would be moral and immoral at the same time, according to the point of view from which we look at it. That action which is moral for a brute-man, would be immoral for a highly cultivated man. For a man on the higher rung of the ladder to come down to the lower is to go against evolution, and, therefore, for him such action is immoral; but for a man to rise from the lower stage to stand on that same rung is moral, because it is in the line of his evolution. So that two persons may well stand on the same rung of the ladder, but the one, having gone upwards and the other having come downwards to reach it, the action for the one is moral and for the other is immoral. Realise that and we shall begin to find our law.

You have two boys: one of them is a clever and intellectual boy, but is very fond of the gratifications of the body, very fond of food and of anything that gives him sensuous pleasure. The other boy shows some dawning spirituality, is bright, quick and intellectual. We will take a third boy who shows the spiritual nature unfolded to a considerable extent. Here are three boys. What motive shall we use to help on the evolution of each? We go to the young man who is very fond of sensual pleasure. If I say to him: "My son, your life should be a life of perfect unselfishness, you should lead an ascetic life," he will shrug his shoulders and go away; and I shall not have helped him up a single rung of the ladder. If I say to him: "My lad, these pleasures of yours are pleasures which give you momentary delight but they will ruin your body and shatter your health; look on that prematurely old man, who has led a life of sensual indulgence; that will be your fate if you go on thus; will it not be better to give a part of your time to the cultivation of your mind, to learning something, so that you may be able to write a book or compose a poem, or help on some of the world's work? You may earn money and get health and fame, and by this attempt you will gratify your ambition; give a rupee now and then to buy a book, instead of buying a dinner". By so addressing him, I stir that youth with an idea of ambition; selfish ambition I admit, but there is not there as yet the power to respond to the appeal for self-sacrifice. The motive of ambition is selfish, but it is selfishness of a higher kind than that sensual gratification, and as it gives him something of the intellect, raises him out of the brute, puts him on the level of the man who is developing the intellect, and thus helps him to rise higher in the scale of evolution, that is a wiser teaching for him than the impracticable selflessness. It gives him not a perfect ideal, but an ideal suited to his capacity.

But when I come to my intellectual youth with dawning spirituality, I shall put before him the ideal of serving his country, of serving India; I shall make this his object and aim, partly selfish and partly unselfish, thus widening his ambition and helping on his evolution. And when I come to the youth of spiritual nature, I will drop all lower motives, and appeal, on the contrary, to the eternal law of self-sacrifice, to devotion to the one Life, the worship of the great Ones and of God. I shall teach Discrimination and Dispassion, and thus help the spiritual nature to unfold its infinite possibilities. Thus understanding morality as relative, we are able to work effectively. If we fail to help every soul, in its own place, it is because we are ill-trained teachers.

In every nation, there are certain definite things which are marked as wrong, such as murder, theft, lying, vileness. All these are recognised as crimes. That is the general view. But it is not wholly borne out by facts. How far are these things recognised as moral and how far as immoral in practice? Why are they recognised as wrong? Because the masses of the nation have reached a certain stage of evolution. Because the majority of the nation are at about the same level of growth, and at that level they recognise these things as evil, as against progress. The result is that the minority, being below this stage, is regarded as being made up of "criminals". The majority has reached a higher stage of evolution, and the majority makes the law; then those who cannot come up even to the lowest level of the majority are dubbed criminals. Two types of criminals present themselves to our view. One type upon which we cannot make any impression by appealing to their sense of right and wrong. They are spoken of by the ignorant public as hardened criminals. But this view is a mistaken one, and leads to lamentable results. They are merely ignorant, ungrown souls, child-souls, infants in the School of Life, and we do not help them to grow by trampling them down and brutalizing them further, because they are scarcely a grade removed from the brute. We should use all the means in our power, all that our reason can suggest, to guide and teach these child-souls, to discipline them into a better life; let us not treat them as hardened criminals because they are mere babies in the nursery.

The other type of criminals is made up of those who feel a certain amount of remorse and repentance after the commission of a crime, who know that they have done wrong. They stand on a higher level, and can he helped to resist evil in future by the very suffering imposed on them by human law. I spoke of the necessity of all experience, in order that the soul might learn to discern between right and wrong. We need experience of good and evil, until we can discriminate the good from the evil, *but no further*. The moment the two lines of actions are distinct before you, and you know that the one is right and the other is wrong, then if you choose the wrong road you are committing sin, you are going against a law that you know and admit. A man at this stage commits sin, because his desires are strong, prompting him to choose the path which is wrong. He suffers, and it is well that he should suffer, if he follows these desires. The moment the knowledge of wrong is present, there at the moment also there is deliberate degradation in yielding to the impulse. Experience of the wrong is only needed before the wrong is recognised as wrong, and in order that it may come to he so recognised. When two courses are before a man, neither of which appears to him to be morally different from the other, then he may take either of those courses and commit it no wrong. But the moment a thing is known to be wrong, it is a treason to ourselves to allow the brute in us to overpower the God in us. That is what is really sin; that is what is the condition of most, but not all, wrong-doers today.

Let us pass front that and look at some particular faults a little more closely. Take murder: we find that the common sense of the community makes a distinction between killing and killing. If a man takes up a knife in anger and stabs his enemy, the law calls him a murderer and hangs him. If a thousand men take up knives and stab a thousand men, then the killing is called war. Glory and not punishment is awarded to him who thus kills. The same crowd who hoot the murderer of one enemy, cheer the men who have killed ten thousand enemies. What is this strange anomaly? How can we explain it? Is there anything to justify the verdict of the community? Is there any distinction between the two acts, which justifies the difference of treatment? There is. War is a thing against which the public conscience more and more protests, and in a moment we shall have to look at this fact of the growth of the public conscience. But while we should do all we can to prevent war, should try to spread peace and to educate our children in the love of peace, there is none the less a real distinction in the conduct of one who kills through private malice, and the killing which takes place in war; this difference is so far-reaching, that I shall dilate upon it a little. In the one case, a personal grudge is satisfied, and personal satisfaction is found. In the other case, one man in killing the other man is not gratifying a personal feeling, is serving no personal object, is seeking no personal gain. The men are killing each other as an act of obedience to a command laid on them by their superiors, whose is the responsibility for the righteousness of the war. All my life I have preached peace, and I have striven to show the evils of war. But, none the less, I recognise that there is much in the mere discipline of the military force, which is of vital importance to those who are subjected to that training. What does the soldier learn? He learns obedience to order, cleanliness, quickness, accuracy, promptness in action, and willingness to undergo physical hardship without complaint or murmur. He learns to risk his life, and to give it for an ideal cause. Is not that a training which has its place in the evolution of the soul? Does not the soul profit by this training? When the ideal of the country fires the heart, when life is sacrificed for it gladly by rough, common and uneducated men, they may be rude, violent, drunken, but they are passing through a training which, in lives to come, will make them better and nobler men.

Then take a phrase used by an Englishman of somewhat strange genius, Rudyard Kipling, who makes soldiers say that they will fight "for the widow at Windsor". That may sound a little rough, but it is well for the man who starves, who suffers mutilation on the battlefield, if he sees before him his Queen-Empress, mother of millions of people, and offers up his life to her, learning for the first time the beauty of fidelity, of courage and devotion. There is the distinction which, very dimly grasped by the public, marks the distinction between private killing and war. For the interest of the one is personal; that of the other belongs to a wider self - the self of the nation.

In dealing with this question of morality, we fall often practically below that view. There are many cases of theft, of lying, of killing, that the law of man does not punish, but that the law of karma notes and brings back to the doer. Many an act of theft is disguised as commerce; many an act of cheating is disguised as trade; many a fine arrangement of lies is classified as diplomacy. Crime reappears under startling forms, disguised and hidden, and men have to learn self-purification in life after life. Then comes in another consideration, before we come to the essence of sin - one which I cannot entirely overpass - thought and action. There are some actions which a man commits, which are inevitable. You do not understand what you are doing, when you allow yourself to think along a line of wrong. You covet in thought another man's gold; you are grasping with your mind's hands, at every moment, what is not yours. You are building the Dharma of the thief. The inner nature, the interior nature, is Dharma, and if you build that inner nature by thoughts that are evil, you will be born with the Dharma that will carry you to deeds of vice. Those deeds will then be done without thought. Have you any idea how many thoughts in you have already gone towards the making of an action? You may dam up water, and prevent it from flowing along a channel, but the moment a hole is made in the dam, the pent-up water will flow through the hole and sweep the dam away: so is it with thought and action. Thought accumulates slowly behind the dam of absence of opportunity. As you think and think, the stream of thought grows fuller and fuller behind the breastwork of circumstances. In another life that breastwork of circumstances gives way, and the action is committed before any new thought has occurred. Those are the inevitable crimes, which sometimes blast a great career, when the thought of the past finds its fruitage in the present, when the karma of accumulated thought comes forth as action. If the opportunity comes to you, and you have time to pause, time to say: "Shall I do it?" then that action is not inevitable for you. The pause for thought means that you can put the thought on the other side and so strengthen the barrier. There is no excuse for doing an action which you have thought of as wrong. Those actions only are inevitable which are done without thinking, where the thought belongs to the past and the action to the present.

We come now to the great question of separateness: there lies in every deed the essence of wrong. In the past, separateness was right. The great course of the divine life-stream was dividing itself into multiplicity; it was needed to build up individual centers of consciousness. So long as a centre needs strengthening, separateness is on the side of progress. Souls at one period need to be selfish; they cannot do without selfishness in the early stages of growth. But now the law of progressing life for the more advanced is the outgrowing of separateness, and the seeking to realise unity. We are now on the path towards unity; we are approaching nearer and nearer to each other. We must now unite, in order to grow further. The purpose is the same, though the method has changed in the evolution through the ages. The public conscience is beginning to recognise that not in separateness but in unity, there lies the true growth of a nation. We are trying to substitute arbitration for war, co-operation for competition, protection of the weak for trampling them under foot, and all this, because the line of evolution now goes towards unity and not towards separateness. Separation is the mark of descent into matter, and unification is the mark of the ascent to Spirit. The world is on the upward trend, although thousands of souls may lag behind. The ideal now is peace, co-operation, protection, brotherhood and helpfulness. The essence of sin now lies in separateness.

But that thought leads us on to another test of conduct. Is the action we are doing one which seeks our own gain, or which helps on the general good? Is our life a self-seeking, useless life, or does it help humanity? If it is selfish, then it is wrong, it is evil, it is against the growth of the world. If you be among those who have seen the beauty of the ideal of unity, and have recognised the perfection of the divine manhood that we seek, then you should kill out this heresy of separateness in yourself.

When we look at much of the teaching of the past and see the conduct of the Sages, certain questions in morality arise, which some find it rather hard to answer. I raise this here, because I may suggest to you the line of thought by which you may defend the Shastras from carping critics and which may enable you to profit by their teachings, without becoming confused. A great Sage is not always, in his conduct, an example that an ordinary man should endeavour to follow. When I speak now of a great Sage, I mean one in whom all personal desire is dead, who is not attracted to any object in the world, whose only life is in obedience to the divine will, who gives himself as one of the channels of divine force for the helping of the world. He performs the functions of a God, and the functions of the Gods differ much from the functions of men. The earth is full of all kinds of catastrophes - wars, earthquakes, famine, pestilences, plagues. Who is their cause? There is no cause in God's universe save God Himself, and these things which seem so terrible, so shocking; so painful, are His ways of teaching us when we are going wrong. A plague sweeps off thousands of the men of a nation. A mighty war scatters its thousands of dead on the field of carnage. Why? Because that nation had disregarded the divine law of its growth, and must learn its lesson by suffering, if it will not learn it by reason. Plague is the result of disregarding the laws of health and of clean living. God is too merciful to permit a law to be disregarded by the whims and fancies and feelings of slowly evolving man, without calling attention to the disregarded. These catastrophes are worked by the Gods, by the agents of Ishvara, who, invisible throughout the world, administer the divine law, as a magistrate administers the civil laws. Just because they are administrators of the law and are acting impersonally, their actions are no more examples for us to follow, than the action of the judge in imprisoning a criminal is an example to show that an ordinary man may take revenge on his enemy. Look, for instance, at the great Sage Narada. We find him stirring up war, when two nations have reached a point where the higher good of each can only be gained by the struggles of war, and by the conquest of one by the other. Bodies are killed, and it is the best help to the men thus slain that their bodies should be struck away, and that, in new bodies, they may have greater possibility of growth. Gods bring about the battle in which thousands of men are slain. It would be wicked for us to imitate them, because to stir up war for the sake of conquest or gain, or ambition, or for some object where personality comes in, is sinful. But in the case of Narada it is not so, because Devarshis such as he is are helping the world along the path of evolution by striking away the obstacles. You will understand something of the wonders and mysteries of the universe, when you know that things that seem evil from the side of form are good from the side of life; all that happens is working for the best. "There is a divinity that shapes our ends, rough-hew them as we may." Religion is right when it says that the Gods rule over the world and guide nations, and lead and even scourge them into the right path when they go astray.

A man, full of personality and attracted by the objects of desire, whose whole self is Kama, such a man, committing an action instigated by Kama, often commits a crime; but the very same action committed by a liberated soul, free from all desire, in carrying out the divine order, would be rightly done. In the utter disbelief that men have fallen into as to the working of thy Gods, such words may seem strange, but there is no energy in nature, which is not the physical manifestation of a God carrying out the will of the Supreme. That is the true view of nature. We see the side of form, and, blinded by Maya, call it evil; but the Gods, as they break up forms, are clearing away every obstacle that obstructs the way of evolution.

We may here understand one or two of those other questions that are often thrown in our faces by those who take a superficial view of things. Supposing a man, who is longing to commit a sin, is prevented from committing it solely by the pressure of circumstances; suppose that the longing is growing stronger and stronger; what is the best thing for him? To have an opportunity to put his longing into action. To commit a crime? Yes, even a crime is less injurious to the soul than a continued brooding over it in the mind, the growing of a cancer at the heart of life. An action once done is dead, and the suffering that follows it teaches the needed lesson, but thought is generative and living.* [* This does not mean that a man should commit a sin rather than struggle against it. So long as he struggles, it is well with him, and he is gaining strength. The case referred to is where there is no struggle, but where the man is longing to do the action and only lacks opportunity. In such case, the sooner the opportunity comes, the better for the man; the pent-up longing breaks forth, the realized wish brings suffering, the man learns a necessary lesson, and is purged of an ever-increasing moral poison.] Do you understand that? If you do, then you will also understand why you find in the scriptures a God putting in the way of a man an opportunity of committing the sin that man is longing to commit, and in fact has committed in his heart. He will suffer, no doubt, for his sin, but he will learn by the suffering that falls on the wrong-doer. Had that evil thought been left to grow in the heart, it would have grown stronger and stronger, and would have gradually wrecked the whole moral nature of the man. For it is like a cancer which, if not speedily removed, will poison the whole body. Far more merciful it is, that such a man should sin and suffer pain, than that he should long to sin and be held back by lack of opportunity merely, and thus make inevitable degradation for lives to come.

So also if a man is making rapid progress, and there is a hidden weakness in him, or some past Karma not exhausted, or evil deed not expiated, that man cannot be liberated while that Karma remains unexhausted, while there is a debt still unpaid. What is the most merciful thing to do? To help that man to pay his debt in anguish and degradation, so that the misery following on the fault may exhaust the Karma of the past. It means that there is swept out of his way an obstacle that prevents his liberation, and God puts that temptation in his way to break the last barrier down. I have not time to work out the details of this most pregnant line of thought, but I ask you to follow it for yourselves and see what it means, and how it illuminates the dark problems of growth, the falls of the saints.

If, when you have assimilated it, you then read such a book as the *Mahabharata,* you will understand the workings of the Gods in the affairs of men; you will see the Gods working in storm and sunshine, in peace and in war, and you will know that it is well with the man and with the nation, whatever may occur to them; for the noblest wisdom and the tenderest love are guiding them to their appointed goal.

I come now to the last word - a word I will dare to speak to you, who have been listening to me patiently on a subject so difficult and abstruse. There is a yet higher note: know that there is a supreme goal, and the last steps on the path to it are not the steps where Dharma can any longer guide us. Let us take some wonderful words from the great Teacher, Shri Krishna, and let us see how in His final instruction, He speaks of something loftier than anything on which we have dared to touch. Here is His message of peace: "Listen thou again to My supreme word, most secret of all; beloved art thou of Me, and steadfast of heart, therefore will I speak for thy benefit. Merge the Manas in Me, be my devotee, sacrifice to Me, prostrate thyself before Me, thou shalt come even to Me. Abandoning all Dharmas, come unto Me alone for shelter; sorrow not, I will liberate thee from all sins" (*Bhagavad-Gita,* xviii, 64-66.).

My last words are addressed only to those who lead here a life of supreme longing to sacrifice themselves to Him; they have a right to these last words of hope and peace. Then the end of Dharma is reached. Then the man desires no longer anything save the Lord. When the soul has reached that stage of evolution, where it asks nothing of the world, but gives itself wholly to God, when it has outgrown all the promptings of desire, when the heart has gained freedom by love, when the whole being throws itself forward at the feet of the Lord - then abandon you all Dharmas; they are no longer for you; no longer for you the law of growth, no longer for you that balancing of duty, no longer for you that scrutiny of conduct. You have given yourself to the Lord. There is nothing left in you that is not divine. What Dharma can any longer remain for you, for, united to Him, you are no longer a separated self. Your life is hid in Him, His life is yours; you may be living in the world, you are but His instrument. You are His wholly. Your life is Ishvara's, and Dharma has no longer any claim on you. Your devotion has liberated you, for your life is hid in God. That is the word of the Teacher. That is the last thought I would leave with you.

And now, my brothers, farewell. Our work together is done. After this imperfect presentation of a mighty subject, may I say to you: listen to the thought in the message, and not to the speaker who is the messenger; open your hearts to the thought, and forget the imperfection of the lips that have spoken it. Remember that, as we climb to God, we must needs try, however feebly, to pass on to our brothers some touch of that life we reach after. Forget therefore the speaker, but remember the teaching. Forget the imperfections which are in the messenger, not in the message. Worship the God whose teaching we have been studying, and pardon in your charity the faults of the servant who has given it utterance.

PEACE TO ALL BEINGS

BOOK TWO
KARMA

PREFACE

FEW words are needed in sending this little book out into the world. It is the fourth of a series of manuals designed to meet the public demand for a simple exposition of theosophical teachings. Some have complained that our literature is at once too abstruse, too technical, and too expensive for the ordinary reader, and it is our hope that the present series may succeed in supplying what is a very real want. Theosophy is not only for the learned; it is for all. Perhaps among those who in these little books catch their first glimpse of its teachings, there may be a few who will be led by them to penetrate more deeply into its philosophy, its science, and its religion, facing its abstruser problems with the student's zeal and the neophyte's ardour. But these manuals are not written for the eager student, whom no initial difficulties can daunt; they are written for the busy men and women of the work-a-day world, and seek to make plain some of the great truths that render life easier to bear and death easier to face. Written by servants of the Masters who are the Elder Brothers of our race, they can have no other object than to serve our fellow-men.

Introduction

EVERY thought of man upon being evolved passes into the inner world, and becomes an active entity by associating itself, coalescing we might term it, with an elemental—that is to say, with one of the semi-intelligent forces of the kingdoms. It survives as an active intelligence—a creature of the mind's begetting—for a longer or shorter period proportionate with the original intensity of the cerebral action which generated it. Thus a good thought is perpetuated as an active, beneficent power, an evil one as a maleficent demon. And so man is continually peopling his current in space with a world of his own, crowded with the offspring of his fancies, desires, impulses and passions; a current which reacts upon any sensitive or nervous organization which comes in contact with it, in proportion to its dynamic intensity. The Buddhist calls it his "Skandha"; the Hindu gives it the name of " Karma". The Adept evolves these shapes consciously; other men throw them off unconsciously.[1]

No more graphic picture of the essential nature of karma has ever been given than in these words, taken from one of the early letters of Master K. H. If these are clearly understood, with all their implications, the perplexities which surround the subject will for the most part disappear, and the main principle underlying karmic action will be grasped. They will therefore be taken as indicating the best line of study, and we shall begin by considering the creative powers of man. All we need as preface is a clear conception of the invariability of law, and of the great planes in Nature.

I. The Invariability of Law

That we live in a realm of law, that we are surrounded by laws that we cannot break, this is a truism. Yet when the fact is recognized in a real -and vital way, and when it is seen to be a fact in the mental and moral world as much as in the physical, a certain sense of helplessness is apt to overpower us, as though we felt ourselves in the grip of some mighty power, that, seizing us, whirls us away whither it will. The very reverse of this is in reality the case, for the mighty power, when it is

---

[1] The Occult World, pp. 89, 90, Fourth Edition.

understood, will obediently carry us whither we will: all forces in Nature can be used in proportion as they are understood—

" Nature is conquered by obedience "—and her resistless energies are at our bidding as soon as we, by knowledge, work with them and not against them. We can choose out of her boundless stores the forces that serve our purpose in momentum, in direction, and so on, and their very invariability becomes the guarantee of our success.

On the invariability of law depends the security of scientific experiment, and all power of planning a result and of predicting the future. On this the chemist rests, sure that Nature will ever respond in the same way, if he be precise in putting his questions. A variation in his results is taken by him as implying a change in his procedure, not a change in Nature. And so with all human action; the more it is based on knowledge, the more secure is it in its forecastings, for all " accident" is the result of ignorance, and is due to the working of laws whose presence was unknown or overlooked. In the mental and moral worlds, as much as in the physical, results can be foreseen, planned for, calculated on. Nature never betrays us; we are betrayed by our own blindness. In all worlds increasing knowledge means increasing power, and omniscience and omnipotence are one.

That law should be as invariable in the mental and moral worlds as in the physical is to be expected, since the universe is the emanation of the ONE, and what we call Law is but the expression of the Divine Nature. As there is one Life emanating all, so there is one Law sustaining all; the worlds rest on this rock of the Divine Nature as on a secure, immutable foundation.

II. The Planes of Nature

To study the workings of karma on the line suggested by the Master, we must gain a clear conception of the three lower planes, or regions, of the universe, and of the principles related to them. The names given to them indicate the state of the consciousness working on them. In this a diagram may help us, showing the planes with the principles related to them, and the vehicles in which a conscious entity may visit them. In practical occultism the student learns to visit these planes, and by his own investigations to transform theory into knowledge. The lowest vehicle, the gross body, serves the consciousness for its work on the physical plane, and in this the consciousness is limited within the capacities of the brain. The term subtle body covers a variety of astral bodies, respectively suitable to the varying conditions of the very complicated region indicated by the name psychic plane. On the devachanic plane there are two well-defined levels, the form level and the formless level; on the lower, consciousness uses an artificial body, the mayavi rupa, but the term Mind Body seems suitable as indicating that the matter of which it is composed belongs to the plane of manas. On the formless level the causal body must be used. Of the buddhic plane it is needless to speak. Now the matter on these planes is not the same, and speaking generally, the matter of each plane is denser than that of the one above it. This is according to the analogy of Nature, for evolution in its downward course is from rare to dense, from subtle to gross. Further, vast hierarchies of beings inhabit these planes, ranging from the lofty intelligences of the spiritual region to the lowest sub-conscious elementals of the physical world. On every plane spirit and matter are conjoined in every particle—-every particle having matter as its body, spirit as its life—and all independent aggregations of particles, all separated forms of every kind, of every type, are ensouled by these living beings, varying in their grades according to the grade of the form. No form exists which is not thus ensouled, but the informing entity may be the loftiest intelligence, the lowest elemental, or any of the countless hosts that range between.

ATMA			
Sushuptic		Buddhi	Vehicles Spiritual Body
Devachanic		Manas	Vehicle Mind Body Causal Body
Psychic or Astral	Higher Psychic	Kama-Manas	Vehicle
	Lower Psychic	Kama	Suble Body
Physical		Linga Sharira Sthula Sharira	Vehicle Etheric Double Gross Body

The entities with which we shall presently be concerned are chiefly those of the psychic plane, for these give to man his body of desire (kama rupa)—his body of sensation, as it is often called—-are indeed built into its astral matrix and vivify his astral senses. They are, to use the technical name, the form elementals (rupa devatas) of the animal world, and are the agents of the changes which transmute vibrations into sensations. The most salient characteristic of the kamic elementals is sensation, the power of not only answering to vibrations but of feeling them; and the psychic plane is crowded with these entities, of varying degrees of consciousness, who receive impacts of every kind and combine them into sensations. Any being who possesses, then, a body into which these elementals are built, is capable of feeling, and man feels through such a body. A man is not conscious in the particles of his body or even in its cells; they have a consciousness of their own, and by this carry on the various processes of his vegetative life; but the man whose body they form does not share their consciousness, does not consciously help or hinder them as they select, assimilate, secrete, build up, and could not at any moment so put his consciousness into rapport with the consciousness of a cell in his heart as to say exactly what it was doing. His consciousness functions normally on the psychic plane; and even in the higher psychic regions, where mind is working, it is mind intermingled with kama, pure mind not functioning on this astral plane.

The astral plane is thronged with elementals similar to those which enter into the desire body of man, and which also form the simpler desire body of the lower animal. By this department of his nature man comes into immediate relations with these elementals, and by them he forms links with all the objects around him that are either attractive or repulsive to him. By his will, by his emotions, by his desires, he influences these countless beings, which sensitively respond to all the thrills of feeling that he sends out in every direction. His own desire body acts as the apparatus, and just as it combines the vibrations that come from without into feelings, so does it dissociate the feelings that arise within into vibrations.

III. The Generation of Thought-Forms

We are now in a position to more clearly understand the Master's words. The mind, working in its own region, in the subtle matter of the higher psychic plane, generates images, thought-forms. Imagination has very accurately been called the creative faculty of the mind, and it is so in a more literal sense than many may suppose who use the phrase. This image-making capacity is the characteristic power of the mind, and a word is only a clumsy attempt to partially represent a mental picture. An idea, a mental image, is a complicated thing, and needs perhaps a whole sentence to describe it accurately, so a salient incident in it is seized, and the word naming this incident imperfectly represents the whole; we say "triangle", and the word calls up in the hearer's mind a picture, which would need a long description if fully conveyed in words; we do our best thinking in symbols, and then laboriously and imperfectly summarize our symbols into words. In regions where mind speaks to mind there is perfect expression, far beyond anything words may convey; even in thought transference of a limited kind it is not words that are sent, but ideas. A speaker puts into words such part of his mental pictures as he can, and these words call up in the hearer's mind pictures corresponding to those in the mind of the speaker; the mind deals with the pictures, the images, not with the words, and half the controversies and misunderstandings that arise come about because people attach different images to the same words, or use different words to represent the same images.

A thought-form, then, is a mental image, created-—• or moulded— by the mind out of the subtle matter of the higher psychic plane, in which, as above said, it works. This form, composed of the rapidly vibrating atoms of the matter of that region, sets up vibrations all around it; these vibrations will give rise to sensations of sound and colour in any entities adapted to translate them thus, and as the thought-form passes outward—or sinks downward, whichever expression may be preferred to express the transition—into the denser matter of the lower psychic regions, these vibrations thrill out as a singing-colour in every direction, and call to the thought form whence they proceed the elementals belonging to that colour.

All elementals, like all things else in the universe, belong to one or other of the seven primary Rays, the seven primeval Sons of Light. The white light breaks forth from the Third LOGOS, the manifested Divine Mind, in the seven Rays, the " Seven Spirits that are before the Throne," and each of these Rays has its seven sub-rays, and so onwards in sequential sub-divisions. Hence, amid the endless differentiations that make up a universe, there are elementals belonging to the various subdivisions, and they are communicated with in a colour-language, grounded on the colour to which they belong. This is why the real knowledge of sounds and colours and numbers —number underlying both sound and colour—has ever been so carefully guarded, for the will speaks to the elementals by these, and knowledge gives power to control.

Master K.H. speaks very plainly on this colour language. He says:

How could you make yourself understood, command in fact, those semi-intelligent Forces, whose means of communicating with us are not through spoken words, but through sounds and colours, in correlations between the vibrations of the two? For sound, light and colour are the main factors in forming those grades of intelligences, those beings of whose very existence you have no conception, nor are you allowed to believe in them—Atheists and Christians, Materialists and Spiritualists, all bringing forward their respective arguments against such a belief-—Science objecting stronger than either of these to such a degrading superstition. *(The Occult World, p. 100)*

Students of the past may remember obscure allusions now and again made to a language of colours; they may recall the fact that in ancient Egypt sacred manuscripts were written in colours, and that mistakes made in the copying were punished with death. But I must not run down this fascinating byway. We are only concerned with the fact that elementals are addressed by colours, and that colour-words are as intelligible to them as spoken words are to men.

The hue of the singing-colour depends on the nature of the motive inspiring the generator of the thought-form. If the motive be pure, loving, beneficent in its character, the colour produced will summon to the thought-form an elemental, which will take on the characteristics impressed on the form by the motive, and act along the line thus traced; this elemental enters into the thought-form, playing to it the part of a soul, and thus an independent entity is made in the astral world, an entity of a beneficent character. If the motive, on the other hand, be impure, revengeful, maleficent in its character, the colour produced will summon to the thought-form an elemental which will equally take on the characteristics impressed on the form by the motive and act along the line thus traced; in this case also the elemental enters into the thought-form, playing to it the part of a soul, and thus making an independent entity in the astral world, an entity of a maleficent character. For example, an angry thought will cause a flash of red, the thought-form vibrating so as to produce red; that flash of red is a summons to the elementals and they sweep in the direction of the summoner, and one of them enters into the thought-form, which gives it an independent activity of a destructive, disintegrating type. Men are continually talking in this colour-language quite unconsciously, and thus calling round them these swarms of elementals, who take up their abodes in the various thought-forms provided; thus it is that a man peoples his current in space with a world of his own, crowded with the offspring of his fancies, desires, impulses and passions. Angels and demons of our own creating throng round us on every side, makers of weal and woe to others, bringers of weal and woe to ourselves—verily, a karmic host.

Clairvoyants can see flashes of colour, constantly changing, in the aura that surrounds every person: each thought, each feeling, thus translating itself in the astral world, visible to the astral sight.. Persons somewhat more developed than the ordinary clairvoyant can also see the thought-forms, and can see the effects produced by the flashes of colour among the hordes of elementals. Activity of Thought-Forms

The life-period of these ensouled thought-forms depends first on their initial intensity, on the energy bestowed upon them by their human progenitor; and secondly on the nutriment supplied to them after their generation, by the repetition of the thought either by him or by others. Their life may be continually reinforced by this repetition, and a thought which is brooded over, which forms the subject of repeated meditation, acquires great stability of form on the psychic plane. So again thought-forms of a similar character are attracted to each other and mutually strengthen each other, making a. form of great energy and intensity, active in this astral world.

Thought-forms are connected with their progenitor by what—for want of a better phrase—we must call a magnetic tie; they react upon him, producing an impression which leads to their reproduction, and in the case mentioned above, where a thought-form is reinforced by repetition, a very definite habit of thought may be set up, a mould may be formed into which thought will readily flow—helpful if it be of a very lofty character, as a noble ideal, but for the most part cramping and a hindrance to mental growth. We may pause for a moment on this formation of habit, as it shows in miniature, in a very helpful way, the working of karma. Let us suppose we could take ready-made a mind, with no past activity behind it— an impossible thing, of course, but the supposition will bring out the special point needed. Such a mind might be imagined to work with perfect freedom and spontaneity, and to produce a thought-form; it proceeds to repeat this many times, until a habit of thought is made, a definite habit, so that the mind will unconsciously slip into that thought, its energies will flow into it without any consciously selective action of the will. Let us further suppose that the mind comes to disapprove this habit of thought, and finds it a clog on its progress; originally due to the spontaneous action of the mind, and facilitating the outpouring of mental energy by providing for it a ready-made channel, it has now become a limitation; but if it is to be gotten rid of, it can only be by the renewed spontaneous action of the mind, directed to the exhaustion and final destruction of this living fetter. Here we have a little ideal karmic cycle, rapidly run through; the free mind makes a habit, and is then obliged to work within that limitation: but it retains its freedom within the limitation and can work against it from within till it wears it out. Of course, we never find ourselves initially free, for we come into the world encumbered with these fetters of our own past making; but the process as regards each separate fetter runs the above round—the mind forges it, wears it, and while wearing it can file it through.

Thought-forms may also be directed by their progenitor towards particular persons, who may be helped or injured by them, according to the nature of the ensouling elemental; it is no mere poetic fancy that good wishes, prayers, and loving thoughts are of value to those to whom they are sent; they form a protective host encircling the beloved, and ward off many an evil influence and danger.

Not only does a man generate and send forth his own thought-forms, but he also serves as a magnet to draw towards himself the thought-forms of others from the astral plane around him, of the classes to which his own ensouled thought-forms belong. He may thus attract to himself large reinforcements of energy from outside, and it lies within himself whether these forces that he draws into his own being from the external world shall be of a good or of an evil kind. If a man's thoughts are pure and noble, he will attract around him hosts of beneficent entities, and may sometimes wonder whence comes to him the power for achievement that seems—and truly seems—to be so much beyond his own. Similarly a man of foul and base thoughts attracts to himself hosts of maleficent entities, and by this added energy for evil commits crimes that astonish him in the retrospect. " Some devil must have tempted me," he will cry; and truly these demoniac forces, called to him by his own evil, add strength to it from without. The elementals ensouling thought-forms, whether these be good or bad, link themselves to the elementals in the man's desire body and to those ensouling his own thought form, and thus work in him, though coming from without. But for this they must find entities of their own kind with which to link themselves, else can they exercise no power. And further, elementals in an opposite kind of thought-form will repel them, and the good man will drive back by his very atmosphere, his aura, all that is foul and cruel. It surrounds him as a protective wall and keeps evil away from him.

There is another form of elemental activity, that brings about widespread results, and cannot therefore be excluded from this preliminary survey of the forces that go to make up karma. Like those just dealt with, this is included in the statement that these thought-forms people the current which reacts upon any sensitive or nervous organization which comes in contact with it, in proportion to its dynamic intensity. To some extent it must affect almost everyone, though the more sensitive the organization the greater the effect. Elementals have a tendency to be attracted towards others of a similar kind—aggregating together in classes, being, in a sense, gregarious on their own account—and when a man sends out a thought-form it not only keeps up a magnetic link with him, but is drawn towards other thought-forms of a similar type, and these congregating together on the astral plane form a good or evil force, as the case may be, embodied in a kind of collective entity. To these aggregations of similar thought-forms are due the characteristics, often strongly marked, of family, local and national opinion; they form a kind of astral atmosphere through which everything is seen, and which colours that to which the gaze is directed, and they react on the desire bodies of the persons included in the group concerned, setting up in them responsive vibrations. Such family, local or national karmic surroundings largely modify the individual's activity, and limit to a very great extent his power of expressing the capacities he may possess. Suppose an idea should be presented to him, he can only see it through this atmosphere that surrounds him, which must colour it and may seriously distort. Here, then, are karmic limitations of a far-reaching kind, that will need further consideration.

The influence of these congregated elementals is not confined to that which they exercise over men through their desire bodies. When this collective entity, as I have called it, is made up of thought-forms of a destructive type, the elementals ensouling these act as a disruptive energy and they often work much havoc on the physical plane. A vortex of disintegrating energies, they are the fruitful sources of "accidents", of natural convulsions, of storms, cyclones, hurricanes, earthquakes, floods. These karmic results will also need some further consideration.

IV. The Making of Karma in Principle

Having thus realized the relation between man and the elemental kingdom, and the moulding energies of the mind—-verily, creative energies, in that they call into being these living forms that have been described —we are in a position to at least partially understand something of the generation and working out of karma during a single life-period. A " life-period", I say, rather than a " life ", because a life means too little if it be used in the ordinary sense of a single incarnation, and it means too much if it be used for the whole life, made up of many stages in the physical body, and of many stages without it. By life-period I mean a little cycle of human existence, with its physical, astral and devachanic experiences, including its return to the threshold of the physical— the four distinct stages through which the soul passes, in order to complete its cycle. These stages are retrodden over and over again during the journey of the eternal pilgrim through our present humanity, and however much the experiences in each such period may vary, both as to quantity and quality, the period will include these four stages for the average human being, and none others.

It is important to realize that the residence outside the physical body is far more prolonged than the residence in it; and the workings of karmic law will be but poorly understood unless the activity of the soul in the non-physical condition be studied. Let us recall the words of a Master, pointing out that the life out of the body is the real one.

The Vedantins, acknowledging two kinds of conscious existence, the terrestrial and the spiritual, point only to the latter as an undoubted actuality. As to the terrestrial life, owing to its changeability and shortness, it is nothing but an illusion of our senses. Our life in the spiritual spheres must be thought an actuality, because it is there that lives our endless, never-changing, immortal I, the Sutratma, . . . This is why we call the posthumous life the only reality, and the terrestrial one, including the personality itself, only imaginary.*(Lucifer, October 1892, art. Life and Death.)*

During earth life, the activity of the soul is most directly manifested in the creation of the thought-forms already described. But in order to follow out with any approach to exactitude the workings of karma, we must now analyse further the term " thought-form", and add some considerations necessarily omitted in the general conception first presented. The soul, working as mind, creates a mental image, the primary " thought-form" (See III); let us take the term mental image to mean exclusively this immediate creation of the mind, and henceforth restrict this term to this initial stage of what is generally and broadly spoken of as a thought-form. This mental image remains attached to its creator, part of the content of his consciousness: it is a living, vibrating form of subtle matter, the Word thought but not yet spoken, conceived but not yet made flesh. Let the reader concentrate his mind for a few moments on this mental image, and obtain a distinct notion of it, isolated from all else, apart from all the results it is going to produce on other planes than its own. It forms, as just said, part of the content of the consciousness of its creator, part of his inalienable property; it cannot be separated from him; he carries it with him during his earthly life, carries it with him through the gateway of death, carries it with him in the regions beyond death; and if, during his upward travelling through those regions, he himself passes into air too rarefied for it to endure, he leaves behind the denser matter built into it, carrying on the mental matrix, the essential form; on his return to the grosser region the matter of that plane is again built into the mental matrix, and the appropriate denser form is reproduced. This mental image may remain sleeping, as it were, for long periods, but it may be re-awakened and revivified, every fresh impulse—from its creator, from its progeny (dealt with below), from entities of the same type as its progeny—increases its life-energy, and modifies its form.

It evolves, as we shall see, according to definite laws, and the aggregation of these mental images makes the character; the outer mirrors the inner, and as cells aggregate into the tissues of the body and are often much modified in the process, so do these mental images aggregate into the characteristics of the mind, and often undergo much modification. The study of the working out of karma will throw much light on these changes. Many materials may enter into the making of these mental images by the creative powers of the soul; it may be stimulated into activity by desire (kama), and may shape the image according to the prompting of passion or of appetite; it may be Self-motivated to a noble ideal, and mould the image accordingly; it may be led by purely intellectual concepts, and form the image thereafter. But lofty or base, intellectual or passional, serviceable or mischievous, divine or bestial, it is always in man a mental image, the product of the creative soul, and on its existence individual karma depends. Without this mental image there can be no individual karma linking life-period to life-period: the manasic quality must be present to afford the permanent element in which individual karma can inhere. The non-presence of manas in the mineral, vegetable, and animal kingdoms has as its corollary the non-generation of individual karma, stretching through death to rebirth. Let us now consider the primary thought-form in .relation to the secondary thought-form, the thought-form pure and simple in relation to the ensouled thought-form, the mental image in relation to the astro-mental image, or the thought-form in the lower astral plane. How is this produced and what is it? To use the symbol employed above, it is produced by the Word-thought becoming the Word-outspoken; the soul breathes out the thought, and the sound makes form in astral matter; as the Ideas in the Universal Mind become the manifested universe when they are outbreathed, so do these mental images in the human mind, when outbreathed, become the manifested universe of their creator. He peoples his current in space with a world of his own. The vibrations of the mental image set up similar vibrations in the denser astral matter, and these cause the secondary thought-form, what I have called the astro-mental image; the mental image itself remains, as has been already said, in the consciousness of its creator, but its vibrations passing outside that consciousness reproduce its form in the denser matter of the lower astral plane. This is the form that affords the casing for a portion of elemental energy, specializing it for the time that the form persists, since the manasic element in the form gives a touch of individuality to that which ensouls it. [How marvellous and how illuminating are the correspondences in Nature!] This is the active entity, spoken of in the Master's description, and it is this astro-mental image that ranges over the astral plane, keeping up with its progenitor (see III and diagram p.46) the magnetic tie spoken of, reacting on its parent, the mental image, and acting also on others. The life-period of an astro-mental image may be long or short, according to circumstances, and its perishing does not affect the persistence of its parent; any fresh impulse given to the latter will cause it to generate afresh its astral counterpart as each repetition of a word produces a new form.

The vibrations of the mental image do not only pass downwards to the lower astral plane, but they pass upwards also into the spiritual plane above it.[2] And as the vibrations cause a denser form on the lower plane, so do they generate a far subtler form—dare I call it form? it is no form to us —on the higher, in the akasha, the world-stuff emanated from the LOGOS Itself. The akasha is the storehouse of all forms, the treasure house whereinto are poured—from the infinite wealth of the Universal Mind—the rich stores of all the Ideas that are to be bodied forth in a given cosmos; thereinto also enter the vibrations from the cosmos—from all the thoughts of all intelligences, from all the desires of all kamic entities, from all the actions performed on every plane by all forms. All these make their respective impressions, the to us formless, but to lofty spiritual intelligences the formed, images of all happenings, and these akashic images—as we will henceforth call them—abide for evermore, and are the true karmic records, the Book of the Lipika,[3] that may be read by any who possess the " opened eye of Dangma." [4] It is the reflection of these akashic images that may be thrown upon the screen of astral matter by the action of the trained attention— as a picture may be thrown on a screen from a slide in a magic-lantern—so that a scene from the past may be reproduced in all its living reality, correct in every detail of its far-off happening; for in the akashic records it exists, imprinted there once for all, and a fleeting living picture of any page of these records can be made at pleasure, dramatized on the astral plane, and lived in by the trained Seer. If this

---

[2] These words downwards and upwards are very misleading; the planes of course interpenetrate each other.
[3] The Secret Doctrine, i, 157-159
[4] Ibid., stanza i, of the Book of Dzyan, and see Conclusion

imperfect description be followed by the reader, he will be able to form for himself some faint idea of karma in its aspect as cause. In the akasha will be pictured the mental image created by a soul, inseparable from it; then the astro-mental image produced by it, the active ensouled creature, ranging the astral plane and producing innumerable effects, all accurately pictured in connection with it, and, therefore, traceable to it and through it to its parent, each such thread—spun as it were out of its own substance by the astro-mental image, as a spider spins its web— being recognizable by its own shade of colour; and however many such threads may be woven into an effect, each thread is distinguishable and is traceable to its original forth-giver, the soul that generated the mental image. Thus, for our clumsy earth-bound intelligences, in miserably inadequate language, we may figure forth the way in which individual responsibility is seen at a glance by the great Lords of karma, the administrators of karmic law; the full responsibility of the soul for the mental image it creates, and the partial responsibility for its far-reaching effects, greater or less as each effect has other karmic threads entering into its causation. Thus also may we understand why motive plays a part so predominant in the working out of karma, and why actions are so relatively subordinate in their generative energy; why karma works out on each plane according to its constituents, and yet links the planes together by the continuity of its thread.

When the illuminating concepts of the wisdom-religion shed their flood of light over the world, dispersing its obscurity and revealing the absolute justice which is working under all the apparent incongruities, inequalities and accidents of life, is it any wonder that our hearts should go out in gratitude unspeakable to the Great Ones-—blessed be they!—• who hold up the torch of truth in the murky darkness, and free us from the tension that was straining us to breaking point, the helpless agony of witnessing wrongs that seemed irremediable, the hopelessness of justice, the despair of love?

Ye are not bound! the Soul of Things is sweet,

The Heart of Being is celestial rest;

Stronger than Woe is will: that which was Good

Doth pass to Better—Best.

Such is the Law which moves to righteousness,

Which none at last can turn aside or stay;

The heart of it is Love, the end of it

Is Peace and Consummation sweet. Obey.

We may perhaps gain in clearness if we tabulate the threefold results of the activity of the Soul that go to the making up of karma as cause, regarded in principle rather than in detail. Thus we have during a life-period:

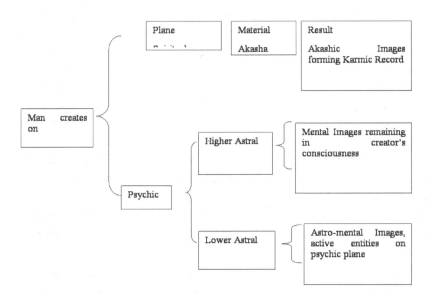

The results of these will be tendencies, capacities, activities, opportunities, environment, etc., chiefly in future life-periods, worked out in accordance with definite laws.

The Making of Karma in Detail

The soul in man, the ego, the maker of karma, must be recognized by the student as a growing entity, a living individual, who increases in wisdom and in mental stature as he treads the path of his aeonian evolution; and the fundamental identity of the higher and lower manas must be constantly kept in mind. For convenience sake we distinguish between them, but the difference is a difference of functioning activity and not of nature: the higher manas is manas working on the spiritual plane, in possession of its full consciousness of its own past; the lower manas is manas working, on the psychic or astral plane, veiled in astral matter, vehicled in kama, and with all its activities intermingled with and coloured by the desire nature; it is to a great extent blinded by the astral matter that veils it, and is in possession only of a portion of the total manasic consciousness, this portion consisting—• for the vast majority—of a limited selection from the more striking experiences of the one incarnation then in progress. For the practical purpose of life as seen by most people, the lower manas is the "!" and is what we term the Personal-Ego; the voice of conscience, vaguely and confusedly regarded as supernatural, as the voice of God, is for them the only manifestation of the higher manas on the psychic plane, and they quite rightly regard it as authoritative, however mistaken they may be as to its nature. But the student must realize that the lower manas is one with the higher, as the ray is one with its sun; the sun-manas shines ever in the heaven of the spiritual plane, the ray-manas penetrates the psychic plane; but if they be regarded as two, otherwise than for convenience in distinguishing their functioning, hopeless confusion will arise.

The ego then is a growing entity, an increasing quantity. The ray sent down is like a hand plunged into water to seize some object and then withdrawn, holding the object in its grasp. The increase in the Ego depends on the value of the objects gathered by its outstretched hand, and the importance of all its work when the ray is withdrawn is limited and conditioned by the experiences gathered while that ray has been functioning on the psychic plane. It is as though a labourer went out into a field, toiling in rain and in sunshine, in cold and in heat, returning home at night; but the labourer is also the proprietor, and all the results of his labour fill his own granaries and enrich his own store. Each Personal-Ego is the immediately effective part of the continuing or Individual-Ego, representing it in the lower world, and necessarily more or less developed according to the stage at which the Ego, as a totality or an individual, has arrived. If this be clearly understood the sense of injustice to the Personal-Ego in its succession to its karmic inheritance -—often felt as a difficulty by the young student of Theosophy—will disappear; for it will be realized that the Ego that made the karma reaps the karma, the labourer that sowed the seed gathers in the harvest, though the clothes in which he worked as sower may have worn out during the interval between the sowing and the reaping; the Ego's astral garments have also fallen to pieces between seed time and harvest, and he reaps in a new suit of clothes; but it is " he " who sowed and who reaps, and if he sowed but little seed or seed badly chosen, it is he who will find but a poor harvest when as reaper he goeth forth.

In the early stages of the Ego's growth his progress will be extremely slow,[5] for he will be led hither and thither by desire, following attractions on the physical plane; the mental images he generates will be mostly of the passional class, and hence the astro-mental images will be violent and short-lived rather than strong and far-reaching. According as manasic elements enter into the composition of the mental image will be the endurance of the astro-mental. Steady, sustained thought will form clearly defined mental images, and correspondingly strong and enduring astro-mental images, and there will be a distinct purpose in the life, a clearly recognized ideal to which the mind is constantly recurring and on which it continually dwells: this mental image will become a dominating influence in the mental life, and the energies of the soul will be largely directed by it.

Let us now study the making of karma by way of the mental image. During a man's life he forms an innumerable assemblage of mental images; some are strong, clear, continually reinforced by repeated mental impulses; others are weak, vague, just formed and then as it were forsaken by the mind; at death the soul finds itself possessed of myriads of these mental images, and they vary in character as well as in strength and definiteness. Some are of spiritual aspirations, longings to be of service, gropings after knowledge, vows of self-dedication to the higher life; some are purely intellectual, clear gems of thought, receptacles of the results of deep study; some are emotional and passional, breathing love, compassion, tenderness, devotion, anger, ambition, pride, greed; some are from bodily appetites, stimulated by uncurbed desire, and represent thoughts of gluttony, drunkenness, sensuality. Each soul has its own consciousness, crowded with these mental images, the outcome of its mental life; not one thought, however fleeting, but is there represented; the astro-mental images may in many cases long have perished, may have had strength enough to endure but for a few hours, but the mental images remain among the possessions of the soul, not one is lacking. All these mental images the

---

[5] See Birth and Evolution of the Soul.

soul carries away with it, when it passes through death into the astral world.

The kama loka, or place of desire, is divided into many strata as it were, and the soul just after death is encumbered with its complete body of desire, or kama rupa, and all the mental images formed by kama-manas that are of a gross and animal nature are powerful on the lowest levels of this astral world. A poorly developed soul will dwell on these images and act them out, thus preparing itself to repeat them again physically in its next life; a man who has dwelt on sensual thoughts and made such mental images will not only be drawn to earth scenes connected with sensual gratifications, but will constantly be repeating them as actions in his mind, and so setting up in his nature stronger and stronger impulses towards the future commission of similar offences. So with other mental images formed from material supplied by the desire-nature, that belong to other levels in kama loka. As the soul rises from the lower levels to the higher, the mental images built from the materials of the lower levels lose these elements, thus becoming latent in consciousness, or what H. P. Blavatsky used to call " privations of matter ", capable of existing but out of material manifestation. The kama-rupic vesture is purified of its grosser elements as the Lower Ego is drawn upwards, or inwards, towards the deva-chanic region, each cast-off "shell" disintegrating in due course, until the last is doffed and the ray is completely withdrawn, free from all astral encasement. On the return of the Ego towards earth-life, these latent images will be thrown outwards and will attract to themselves the appropriate kamic materials, which make them capable of manifestation on the astral plane, and they will become the appetites, passions and lower emotions of his desire-body for his new incarnation.

We may remark in passing that some of the mental images encircling the newly arrived soul are the source of much trouble during the earlier stages ot the postmortem life; superstitious beliefs presenting themselves as mental images torture the soul with pictures of horrors that have no place in its real surroundings.[6]

---

[6] See The Astral Plane, C. W. Leadbeater, pp. 45, 46

All the mental images formed from the passions and appetites are subjected to the process above described, to be remanifested by the ego on its return to earth-life, and as the writer of the Astral Plane says:

The LIPIKA, the great Karmic deities of the Kosmos, weigh the deeds of each personality when the final separation of its principles takes place in Kama Loka, and give as it were the mould of the Etheric Double exactly suitable to its Karma for the man's next birth.[7]

Freed for the time from these lower elements, the soul passes on into devachan, where it spends a time proportionate to the wealth or poverty of its mental images pure enough to be carried into that region. Here it finds again every one of its loftier efforts, however brief it may have been, however fleeting, and here it works upon them, building out of these materials powers for its coming lives.

The devachanic life is one of assimilation; the experiences collected on earth have to be worked into the texture of the soul, and it is by these that the ego grows; its development depends on the number and variety of the mental images it has formed during its earth-life, and transmuted into their appropriate and more permanent types. Gathering together all the mental images of a special class, it extracts from them their essence; by meditation it creates a mental organ and pours into it as faculty the essence it has extracted. For instance: a man has formed many mental images out of aspirations for knowledge and efforts to understand subtle and lofty reasonings; he casts off his body, his mental powers being of only average kind; in his devachan he works on all these mental images, and evolves them into capacity, so that his soul returns to earth with a higher mental apparatus than it before possessed, with much increased intellectual powers, able to achieve tasks for which before it was utterly inadequate. This is the transformation of the mental images, by which as mental images they cease to exist; if in later lives the soul would seek to see again these as they were, it must seek them in the karmic records, where they remain for ever as akashic images. By this transformation they cease to be mental images created and worked on by the soul, and become powers of the soul, part of its very nature. If then a man desires to possess higher mental faculties than he at present enjoys, he can ensure their development by deliberately willing to acquire them, persistently

---

[7] See The Astral Plane, C. W. Leadbeater, pp. 86

keeping their acquirement in view, for desire and aspiration in one life become faculty in another, and the will to perform becomes the capacity to achieve. But it must be remembered that the faculty thus built is strictly limited by the materials supplied to the architect; there is no creation out of nothing, and if the soul on earth fails to exercise its powers by sowing the seed of aspiration and desire, the soul in devachan will have but scanty harvest.

Mental images which have been constantly repeated, but are not of the aspiring character, of the longing to achieve more than the feeble powers of the soul permit, become tendencies of thought, grooves into which mental energy runs easily and readily. Hence the importance of not letting the mind drift aimlessly among insignificant objects, idly creating trivial mental images, and letting them dwell in the mind. These will persist and form channels for future outpourings of mental force which will thus be led to meander about on low levels running into the accustomed grooves, as the paths of least resistance.

The will or desire to perform a certain action, such will or desire having been frustrated, not by want of ability but by want of opportunity, or by circumstances forbidding accomplishment, will cause mental images which—if the action be of a high and pure nature— will be acted out in thought on the devachanic plane, and will be precipitated as actions on returning to earth. If the mental image was formed out of desire to do beneficent actions, it would give rise to the mental performance of these actions in devachan; and this performance, the reflection of the image itself, would leave it in the Ego as an intensified 'mental image of an action, which would be thrown out on to the physical plane as a physical act, the moment the touch of favourable opportunity precipitated this crystallization of the thought into the act. The physical act is inevitable when the mental image has been realized as action on the devachanic plane. The same law applies to mental images formed out of baser desires, though these never pass into devachan, but are subjected to the process before described, to be reformed on the way back to earth. Repeated covetous desires, for instance, out of which mental images are formed, will crystallize out as acts of theft, when circumstances are propitious. The causative karma is complete, and the physical act has become the inevitable effect, when it has reached the stage at which another repetition of the mental image means its passing into action. It must not be forgotten that repetition of an act tends to make the act automatic, and this law works on planes other than the physical; if then an action be constantly repeated on the psychic plane it- will become automatic, and when opportunity offers will automatically be imitated on the physical. How often it is said after a crime, " It was done before I thought ", or " If I had thought for a moment I would never have done it"! The speaker is quite right in his plea that he was not then moved by a deliberate thought-out idea, and he is naturally ignorant as to preceding thoughts, the train of causes that led up to the inevitable result. Thus a saturated solution will solidify if but one more crystal be dropped into it; at the mere contact, the whole passes into the solid state. When the aggregation of mental images has reached saturation point, the addition of but one more solidifies them into an act. The act, again, is inevitable, for the freedom of choice has been exhausted in choosing over and over again to make the mental image, and the physical is constrained to obey the mental impulsion. The desire to do in one life reacts as compulsion to do in another, and it seems as though the desire worked as a demand upon Nature, to which she responds by affording the opportunity to perform.[8]

The mental images stored up by the memory as the experiences through which the soul has passed during its earth-life, the exact record of the action upon it of the external world, must also be worked on by the soul. By study of these, by meditation upon them, the soul learns to see their interrelations, their value as translations to it of the workings of the Universal Mind in manifested Nature; in a sentence, it extracts from them by patient thought upon them all the lessons they have to teach—lessons of pleasure and pain, of pleasure breeding pain and pain breeding pleasure, teaching the presence of inviolable laws to which it must learn to conform itself. Lessons of success and failure, of achievement and disappointment, of fears proving groundless, of hopes failing realization, of strength collapsing under trial, of fancied knowledge betraying itself as ignorance, of patient endurance wresting victory from apparent defeat, of recklessness changing into defeat apparent victory. Over all these things the soul ponders, and by its own alchemy it changes all this mixture of experiences into the gold of wisdom, so that it may return to earth as a wiser soul, bringing to bear

---

[8] See the later section on the working out of karma.

on the events which meet it in the new life this result of the experiences of the old. Here again the mental images have been transmuted, and no longer exist as mental images. They can only be recovered in their old form from the karmic records. It is from the mental images of experiences, and more especially from those which tell how suffering has been caused by ignorance of law, that conscience is born and is developed. The soul during its successive earth-lives is constantly led by desire to rush headlong after some attractive object; in its pursuit it dashes itself against law, and falls, bruised and bleeding. Many such experiences teach it that gratifications sought against law are but wombs of pain, and when in some new earth-life the desire-body would fain carry the soul into enjoyment which is evil, the memory of past experiences asserts itself as conscience, and cries aloud its forbiddance, and reins in the hurrying horses of the senses that would plunge heedlessly after the objects of desire. At the present stage of evolution all but the most backward souls have passed through sufficient experiences to recognize the broad outlines of " right " and " wrong," i.e., of harmony with the Divine Nature, and of discord, and on these main questions of ethics a wide and long experience enables the soul to speak clearly and definitely. But on many higher and subtler questions, belonging to the present stage of evolution and not to the stages that lie behind us, experience is still so restricted and insufficient that it has not yet been worked up into conscience, and the soul may err in its decision, however well intentioned its effort to see clearly and to act rightly. Here its will to obey sets it in line with the Divine Nature on the higher planes, and its failure to see how to obey on the lower plane will be remedied for the future by the pain it feels as it blunders up against the law: the suffering will teach it what before it knew not, and its sorrowful experiences will be worked into conscience, to preserve it from similar pain in the future, to give it the joy of fuller knowledge of God in Nature, of self-conscious accord with the Law of Life, of self-conscious co-operation in the work of evolution.

Thus far we see as definite principles of karmic law, working with mental images as causes, that:

Aspirations and Desires become Capacities.

Repeated Thoughts „ Tendencies.

Wills to perform „ Actions.

Experiences ,, Wisdom.

Painful Experiences ,, Conscience.

Karmic law working with astro-mental images seems better considered under the head of the working out of karma, to which we will now turn. The Working out of Karma

When the soul has lived out its devachanic life, and has assimilated all that it can of the material gathered during its last period on earth, it begins to be drawn again towards earth by the links of desire that bind it to material existence. The last stage of its life-period now lies before it, the stage during which it re-clothes itself for another experience of earthly life, the stage that is closed by the gateway of birth.

The soul steps over the threshold of devachan into what has been called the plane of reincarnation, bringing with it the result, small or great, of its devachanic work. If it be but a young soul, it will have gained but little; progress in the early stages of soul evolution is slow to an extent scarcely realized by most students, and during the babyhood of the soul life-day succeeds life-day in wearying succession, each earth life sowing but little seed, each devachan ripening but little fruit. As faculties develop, growth quickens at an ever increasing rate, and the soul that enters devachan with a large store of material, comes out of it with a large increase of faculty, worked out under the general laws before stated. It issues from devachan clothed only in that body of the soul that endures and grows throughout the manvantara, surrounded by the aura that belongs to it as an individual, more or less glorious, many-hued, luminous, definite, and extensive, according to the stage of evolution reached by the soul. It has been wrought in the heavenly fire, and conies forth as King Soma.[9]

Passing on to the astral plane on its earthward journey, it clothes itself anew in a body of desire, the first result of the workings out of its past karma. The mental images formed during the past "from materials supplied by the desire nature, that had become latent in consciousness, or what H. P. Blavatsky used to call 'privations of matter,' capable of existing, but out of material manifestation,"are now thrown outwards by the soul, and immediately attract to themselves from the matter of

---

[9] A mystic name, full of meaning to the student who understands the part played by Soma in some ancient mysteries.

the astral plane the kamic elements congenial to their natures, and "become the appetites, passions, and lower emotions of his [the Ego's] desire body for his new incarnation."[10]

When this work is accomplished —a work sometimes very brief, sometimes one that causes long delay—the Ego stands in the karmic vesture he has prepared for himself, ready to be " clothed upon", to receive from the hands of the agents of the great Lords of Karma the etheric double J built for him according to the elements he has himself provided, after which shall be shaped his physical body, the house which he must inhabit during his coming physical life. The individual and the personal Ego are thus immediately self-built, as it were—-what he thought on, that he has become; his qualities, his " natural gifts ", all these appertain to him as the direct results of his thinking; the man is in very truth self-created, responsible, in the fullest sense of the word, for all that he is.

But this man is to have a physical and etheric body that will largely condition the exercise of his faculties; he is to live in some environment, and according to this will be his outward circumstances; he is to tread a path marked out by the causes he has set going, other than those which appear as effects in his faculties; he has to meet events joyful and sorrowful, resulting from the forces he has generated. Something more than his individual and personal nature seems here to be needed: how is the field to be provided for its energies? How are the conditioning instruments and the reacting circumstances to be found and adapted?

We approach a region whereof little may be fitly said, in that it is the region of mighty spiritual Intelligences, whose nature is far beyond the scope of our very limited faculties, whose existence may indeed be known and whose workings may be traced, but towards whom we stand much in the position occupied by one of the least intelligent lower animals towards ourselves, in that it may know that we exist but can have no conception of the scope and workings of our consciousness. These -Great Ones are spoken of as the Lipika and the Four Maharajahs. How little we can know of the Lipika may be seen from the following:

---

[10] Formerly called the Linga Sharira, a name that gave rise to much confusion.

The Lipika, a description of whom is given in Commentary 6 of Stanza IV, are the Spirits of the Universe. . . . [They] belong to the most Occult portion of cosmogenesis, which cannot be given here. Whether the Adepts—even the highest—know this angelic order in the completeness of its triple degrees, or only the lower one connected with the records of our world, is something which the writer is unprepared to say, and she would rather incline to the latter supposition. Of its highest grade one thing only is taught, the Lipika are connected with Karma—being its direct Recorders.'

They are the " Second Seven ", and they keep the astral records, filled with the akashic images before spoken of. They are connected with the destiny of every man, and the birth of every child.[11]

They give " the mould of the Etheric Double ",[12] which will serve as the type of the physical body suited for the expression of the mental and passional faculties evolved by the Ego that is to dwell therein, and They give it to " The Four "—to the Maharajahs, Who Are the protectors of mankind and also the agents of Karma on Earth.[13]

Of these H. P. Blavatsky, writes further, quoting the Fifth Stanza of the Book of Dzyan:

Four " Winged Wheels at each corner. . . for the Four Holy Ones and Their Armies (Hosts)." These are the " Four Maharajahs," or Great Kings of the Dhyan Chohans, the Devas, Who preside over each of the four cardinal points. . . . These Beings are also connected with Karma as the latter needs physical and material agents to carry out its decrees.

Receiving the mould—once more the " privation of matter"—-from the Lipika, the Maharajahs choose . for the composition of the etheric double the elements suited to the qualities that are to be expressed through it, and this etheric double thus becomes a fitting karmic instrument for the Ego, giving it alike the basis for expression of the faculties it has evolved, and the limitations imposed upon it by its own past failures and wasted opportunities. This mould is guided by the Maharajahs to the country, the race, the family, the social surroundings, which afford the most suitable field for the working out

---

[11] *The Secret Doctrine, i, 131.*

[12] *Ibid, i, 151.*

[13] *Ibid., i. 147*

of the karma allotted to the particular life-span in question, that which the Hindu calls the prarabdha, or beginning, karma; i.e., that which is to be worked out in the opening life-period. In no one life can the accumulated karma of the past be worked out—no one instrument could be formed, no surroundings could be found, suitable for the expression of all the slowly evolved faculties of the Ego, nor affording all the circumstances necessary for reaping all the harvest sown in the past, for discharging all the obligations contracted towards other Egos with whom the incarnating soul has come into contact in the course of its long evolution. So much then of the total karma as can be arranged for in one life-period, has a suitable etheric double provided for it, the mould of that double being guided to a suitable field. It is placed where the Ego may come into relations with some of such Egos, with whom it has been related in its past, as are present in, or are coming into, incarnation during its own life-period. A country is chosen where the religious, political and social conditions can be found which are suitable to some of its capacities, and afford the field for the occurrence of some of the effects it has generated. A race is selected—subject, of course, to the wider laws affecting incarnation in races, into which we cannot here enter—of which the characteristics resemble some of the faculties which are ripe for exercise, of which the type befits the incoming soul. A family is found in which physical heredity has evolved the kind of physical materials which, built into the etheric double, will adapt themselves to its constitution; a family of which the general or special physical organization will afford play to the mental and passional natures of the Ego. Out of the manifold qualities existing in the soul, and out of the manifold physical types existing in the world, such can be selected as are adapted to each other, a suitable casing can be built for the waiting Ego, an instrument and a field in which some of his karma can be out-worked. Fathomless to our short plummet lines as may be the knowledge and the power required for such adaptations, we can yet dimly see that the adaptations can be made, and that perfect justice can be done; the web of a man's destiny may indeed be composed of threads that to us are innumerable, and that may need to be woven into a pattern of to us inconceivable complexity; a thread may disappear —it has only passed to the under side to come to the surface again presently; a thread may suddenly appear —it has only re-emerged on the upper side after a long transit underneath; seeing but a fragment of the web, the pattern may to our short sight be indistinguishable. As was written by the sage Iamblichus:

What appears to us to be an accurate definition of justice does not also appear to be so to the Gods. For we, looking to that which is most brief, direct our attention to things present, and to this momentary life, and the manner in which it subsists. But the Powers that are superior to us know the whole life of the Soul, and all its former lives. (On the Mysteries, iv, 4)

This assurance that " perfect justice rules the world " rinds support from the increasing knowledge of the evolving soul; for as it advances and begins to see on higher planes and to transmit its knowledge to the waking consciousness, we learn with ever-growing certainty, and therefore with ever-increasing joy, that the Good Law is working with undeviating accuracy, that its Agents apply it everywhere with unerring insight, with unfailing strength, and that all is therefore very well with the world and with its struggling souls. Through the darkness rings out the cry, " All is well," from the watchmen souls who carry the lamp of Divine Wisdom through the murky ways of our human city.

Some of the principles of the working out of the Law we can see, and a knowledge of these will help us in the tracing out of causes, the understanding of effects.

We have already seen that Thoughts build Character; let us next realize that Actions make Environment.

Here we have to do with a general principle of far-reaching effect, and it will be well to work it out a little into detail. By his actions man affects his neighbours on the physical plane; he spreads happiness around him, or he causes distress, increasing or diminishing the sum of human welfare. This increase or diminution of happiness may be due to very different motives—good, bad or mixed. A man may do an act that gives widespread enjoyment from sheer benevolence, from a longing to give happiness to his fellow creatures; let us say that from such a motive he presents a park to a town, for the free use of its inhabitants; another may do a similar act from mere ostentation, from desire to attract attention from those who can bestow social honours (say, he might give it as purchase money for a title); a third may give a park from mixed motives, partly unselfish, partly selfish. The motives will severally affect these three men's characters in their future incarnations, for improvement, for degradation, for small results. But the effect of the action in causing happiness to large numbers of people does not depend on the motive of the giver; the people enjoy the park equally, no matter what may have prompted its gift, and this enjoyment, due to the action of the giver, establishes for him a karmic claim on Nature, a debt due to him that will be scrupulously paid. He will receive a physically comfortable or luxurious environment, as he has given widespread physical enjoyment, and his sacrifice of physical wealth will bring him his due reward, the karmic fruit of his action. This is his right; but the use he makes of his position, the happiness he derives from his wealth and his surroundings, will depend chiefly on his character, and here again the just reward accrues to him, each seed bearing its appropriate harvest. Service rendered to the full measure of opportunity in one life will produce, as effect, enlarged opportunities of service in another; thus one who in a very limited sphere helped each who came in the way, would in a future life be born into a position where openings for giving effective help were many and far-reaching.

Again, wasted opportunities reappear transmuted as limitations of the instrument, and as misfortunes in the environment. For instance, the brain of the etheric double will be built defectively, thus bringing about a defective physical brain; the ego will plan, but will find itself lacking in executive ability, or will grasp an idea, but be unable to impress it distinctly on the brain. The wasted opportunities are transformed into frustrated longings, into desires which fail to find expression, into yearnings to help, blocked by the absence of power to render it, whether from defective capacity or from lack of occasion.

This same principle is often at work in the cutting away from tender care of some well-loved child or idolized youth. If an ego treats unkindly or neglects one to whom he owes affectionate duty and protection, or service of any kind, he will but too likely again find himself born in close relationship with the neglected one, and perhaps tenderly attached to him, only for early death to snatch him away from the encircling arms; the despised poor relation may reappear as the much-honoured heir, the only son, and when the parents find their house left unto them desolate, they marvel at the " unequal ways of Providence " that deprive them of their only one, on whom all their hopes have been set, and leave untouched the many children of their neighbour. Yet are the ways of karma equal, though past finding out, save for those whose eyes have been opened.

Congenital defects result from a defective etheric double, and are life-long penalties for serious rebellions against law, or for injuries inflicted upon others. All such arise from the working of the Lords of Karma, and are the physical manifestation of the deformities necessitated by the errors of the Ego, by his excesses and defects, in the mould of the etheric double made by them. So again from their just administration of the Law come the inwrought tendency to reproduce a family disease, the suitable configuration of the etheric double, and the direction of it to a family in which a given disease is hereditary, and which affords the " continuous plasm " suitable to the development of the appropriate germs. The development of artistic faculties—to take another type of quality—will be answered by the Lords of Karma by the provision of a mould for the etheric double after which a delicate nervous system can be physically built, and often by the guiding of it to a family in whose members the special faculty developed by the Ego has found expression, sometimes for many generations. For the expression of such a faculty as that of music, for instance, a peculiar physical body is needed, a delicacy of physical ear and of physical touch, and to such delicacy an appropriate physical heredity would be most conducive.

The rendering of service to man collectively as by some noble book or speech, the spreading of elevating ideas by pen or tongue, is again a claim upon the law, scrupulously discharged by its mighty Agents. Such help given comes back as help bestowed on the giver, as mental and spiritual assistance which is his by right.

We thus may grasp the broad principles of karmic working, the respective parts played by the Lords of Karma and by the Ego itself in the destiny of the individual. The Ego supplies all the materials, but the materials are used by the Lords or by the Ego respectively according to their nature: the latter builds up the character, gradually evolves itself; the former build the mould that limits, choose the environment, and generally adapt and adjust, in order that the good law may find its unerring expression despite the clashing wills of men.

V. Facing Karmic Results

Sometimes people feel, on first recognizing the existence of karma, that if all be the working out of Law they are but helpless slaves of destiny. Before considering how the Law may be utilized for the control of destiny, let us study for a few moments a typical case, and see how necessity and freewill—'to use the accepted terms—are both at work, and at work in harmony.

A man comes into the world with certain inborn mental faculties, let us say of an average type, with a passional nature that shows definite characteristics, some good, some bad; with an etheric double and physical body fairly well-formed and healthy, but of no specially splendid character. These are his limitations, clearly marked out for him, and he finds himself when he reaches manhood with this mental, passional, astral, physical " stock-in-hand ", and he has to do the best he can with it. There are many mental heights that he is definitely unable to climb, mental conceptions which his powers do not permit him to grasp; there are temptations to which his passional nature yields, though he strives against them; there are triumphs of physical strength and skill that he cannot achieve; in fact, he finds that he can no more think as a genius thinks than he can be beautiful as an Apollo. He is within a limiting ring and cannot pass out of it, long as he may for liberty. Moreover, he cannot avoid troubles of many kinds; they strike him, and he can only bear his pain; he cannot escape from it. Now these things are so. The man is limited by his past thoughts, by his wasted opportunities, by his mistaken choices, by his foolish yieldings; he is bound by his forgotten desires, enchained by his errors of an earlier day. And yet he is not bound, the Real Man. He who made the past that imprisons his present, can work within the prison house and create a future of liberty. Nay, let him know that he himself is free, and the fetters will crumble away from his limbs, and according to the measure of his knowledge will be the illusoriness of his bonds. But for the ordinary man to whom the knowledge will come as a spark, not as a flame, the first step towards freedom will be to accept his limitations as self-made and proceed to enlarge them. True, he cannot think as a genius thinks just yet, but he can think to the very best of his ability, and by-and-by he will become a genius; he can make power for the future, and he will. True, he cannot get rid of his passional follies in a moment, but he can fight against them, and when he has failed he can fight on, certain that presently he will conquer. True, he has astral and physical weaknesses and uglinesses, but as his thoughts grow strong and pure and beautiful, and his work beneficent, he is ensuring for himself more perfect forms in days to come. He is always himself, the free soul, in the midst of his prison house, and he can hew down the walls he himself has built. He has no gaoler save himself: he can will his freedom, and in willing it he will achieve.

A trouble meets him; he is bereaved of a friend, he commits a serious fault. Be it so; he sinned as thinker in the past, he suffers as actor in the present. But his friend is not lost; he will hold him fast by love and in the future he will find him again; meanwhile there are others around him to whom he can give the services he would have showered on his beloved, and he will not again neglect the duties that are his and so sow seed for similar loss in future lives. He has committed an open wrong and suffers its penalty, but he thought it in the past, else could he not have wrought it now: he will patiently endure the penalty he purchased by his thought, and will so think today that his morrows shall be free from shame. Into what was darkness has come a ray of light, and the light is singing to him:

Ho! ye who suffer! know

Ye suffer from yourselves. None else compels.

The law that seemed to be fetters has become wings, and by it he can rise to regions of which without it he could only dream.

Building the Future

The crowds of souls drift onwards along the sluggish current of time. As the earth rolls, it carries them with it; as globe succeeds globe, they too pass on. But the wisdom religion is proclaimed anew to the world that all who choose may cease to drift, and may learn to outstrip the slow evolution of the worlds.

The student, when he grasps something of the meaning of the law, of its absolute certainty, of its unerring exactitude, begins to take himself in hand and actively to superintend his own evolution. He scrutinizes his own character, and then proceeds to manipulate it, deliberately practising mental and moral qualities, enlarging capacities, strengthening weaknesses, supplying deficiencies, removing excrescences. Knowing that he becomes that on which he meditates, he deliberately and regularly meditates on a noble ideal, for he understands why the great Christian initiate Paul bade his disciples " think on" the things that are true, honest, just, pure, lovely, and of good report. Daily he will meditate on his ideal; daily he will strive to live it; and he will do this persistently and calmly, " without haste, without rest ", for he knows that he is building on a sure foundation, on the rock of the eternal law. He appeals to the law; he takes refuge in the law; for such a man failure exists not; there is no power in heaven or in earth that can bar his way. During earth life he gathers his experiences, utilizing all that comes in his way; during devachan he assimilates them and plans out his future buildings.

Herein lies the value of a true theory of life, even while the theory rests on the testimony of others and not on individual knowledge. When a man accepts and partially understands the working of karma, he can at once begin this building of character, setting each stone with deliberate care, knowing that he is building for eternity. There is no longer hasty running up and pulling down, working on one plan today, on another tomorrow, on none at all the day after; but there is a drafting of a well thought out scheme of character, as it were, and then the building according to the scheme, for the soul becomes an architect as well as a builder, and wastes no more time in abortive beginnings. Hence the speed with which the later stages of evolution are accomplished, the striking, almost incredible advances, made by the strong soul in its manhood.

VI. Moulding Karma

The man who has set himself deliberately to build the future will realize, as his knowledge increases, that he can do more than mould his own character, thus making his future destiny. He begins to understand that he is at the centre of things in a very real sense, a living, active, self-determining being, and that he can act upon circumstances as well as upon himself. He has long been accustoming himself to follow the great ethical laws, laid down for the guidance of humanity by the Divine Teachers, who have been born from age to age, and he now grasps the fact that these laws are based on fundamental principles in Nature, and that morality is Science applied to conduct. He sees that in his daily life he can neutralize the ill results that would follow from some ill deed, by bringing to bear upon the same point a corresponding force for good. A man sends against him an evil thought; he might meet it with another of its own kind, and then the two thought-forms, running together like two drops of water, would be reinforced, strengthened, each by each. But this one against whom the evil thought is flying is a knower of karma, and he meets the malignant form with the force of compassion and shatters it; the broken form can no longer be ensouled with elemental life; the life melts back to its own, the form disintegrates; its power for evil is thus destroyed by compassion, and " hatred ceases by love". Delusive forms of falsehood go forth into the astral world; the man of knowledge sends against them forms of truth; purity breaks up foulness, and charity selfish greed. As knowledge increases, this action becomes direct and purposive, the thought is aimed with definite intent, winged with potent will. Thus evil karma is checked in its very inception, and naught is left to make a karmic tie between the one who shot a shaft of injury and the one who burned it up by pardon. The Divine Teachers, who spoke as men having authority on the duty of overcoming evil with good, based their precepts on their knowledge of the law; Their followers who obey without fully seeing the scientific foundation of the precept, lessen the heavy karma that would be generated if they answered hate with hate. But men of knowledge deliberately destroy the evil forms, understanding the facts on which the teaching of the Masters has ever been based, and sterilizing the seed of evil, they prevent a future harvest of pain.

At a stage which is comparatively advanced in comparison with that of the slowly drifting, average humanity, a man will not only build his own character and work with deliberate intent on the thought-forms that come in his way, but he will begin to see the past and thus more accurately to gauge the present, tracing karmic causes onwards to their effects. He becomes able to modify the future by consciously setting forces to work, designed to interact with others already in motion. Knowledge enables him to utilize law with the same certainty with which scientists utilize it in every department of Nature.

Let us pause for a moment to consider the laws of motion. A body has been set in motion, and is moving along a definite line; if another force be brought to bear upon it, differing in direction from the one that gave it its initial impulse, the body will move along another line—a line compounded of the two impulses; no energy will be lost, but part of the force which gave the initial impulse will be used up in partially counteracting the new, and the resultant direction along which the body will move will be that neither of the first force nor of the second, but of the interplay of the two. A physicist can calculate exactly at what angle he must strike a moving body in order to cause it to move in a desired direction, and although the body itself may be beyond his immediate reach, he can send after it a force of calculated velocity to strike it at a definite angle, thus deflecting it from its previous course, and impelling it along a new line. In this there is no violation of law, no interference with law; only the utilization of law by knowledge, the bending of natural forces to accomplish the purpose of the human will. If we apply this principle to the moulding of karma, we shall readily see—-apart from the fact that law is inviolable—that there is no "interference with karma", when we modify its action by knowledge. We are using karmic force to affect karmic results, and once more we conquer Nature by obedience.

Let us now suppose that the advanced student, glancing backwards over the past, sees lines of past karma converging to a point of action of an undesirable kind; he can introduce a new force among the converging energies, and so modify the event, which must be the resultant of all the forces concerned in its generation and ripening. For such action he requires knowledge, not only the power to see the past and to trace the lines which connect it with the present, but also to calculate exactly the influence that the force he introduces will exercise as modifying the resultant, and further the effects that will flow from this resultant considered as cause. In this way he may lessen or destroy the results of evil wrought by himself in the past, by the good forces he pours forth into his karmic stream; he cannot undo the past, he cannot destroy it, but so far as its effects are still in the future he can modify them or reverse them, by the new forces he brings to bear as causes taking part in their production. In all this he is merely utilizing the law, and he works with the certainty of the scientist, who balances one force against another and, unable to destroy a unit of energy, can yet make a body move as he will by a calculation of angles and of movements. Similarly karma may be accelerated or delayed, and thus again will undergo modification by the action of the surroundings amid which it is worked out. Let us put the same thing again a little differently, for the conception is an important and a fruitful one. As knowledge grows, it becomes easier and easier to get rid of the karma of the past. Inasmuch as causes which are working out to their accomplishment, all come within the sight of the soul which is approaching its liberation, as it looks back over past lives, as it glances down the vista of centuries along which it has been slowly climbing, it is able to see there the way in which its bonds were made, the causes which it set in motion: it is able to see how many of those causes have worked themselves out and are exhausted, how many of those causes are still working themselves out. It is able not only to look backwards but also to look forwards and see the effects these causes will produce; so that, glancing in front, the effects that will be produced are seen, and glancing behind, the causes that will bring about these effects are also visible. There is no difficulty in the supposition that just as you find in ordinary physical nature that knowledge of certain laws enables us to predict a result, and to see the law that brings that result about, so we can transfer this idea on to a higher plane, and can imagine a condition of the developed soul, in which it is able to see the karmic causes that it has set going behind it, and also the karmic effects through which it has to work in the future.

With such a knowledge of causes, and a vision of their working out, it is possible to introduce fresh causes to neutralize these effects, and by utilizing the law, and by relying absolutely on its unchanging and unvarying character, and by a careful calculation of the force set going, to make the effects in the future those which we desire. That is a mere matter of calculation. Suppose vibrations of hatred have been set going in the past, we can deliberately set to work to quench these vibrations, and to prevent their working out into the present and future, by setting up against them vibrations of love. Just in the same way as we can take a wave of sound, and then a second wave, and setting the two going one slightly after the other, so that the vibrations of the denser part of the one shall correspond to the rarer part of the other, and thus out of sounds we can make silence by interference, so in the higher regions it is possible by love and hate vibrations, used by knowledge and controlled by will, to bring karmic causes to an ending and so to reach equilibrium, which is another word for liberation. That knowledge is beyond the reach of the enormous majority. What the majority can do is this, if they choose to utilize the science of the soul, they may take the evidence of experts on this subject, they may take the moral precepts of the great religious Teachers of the world, and by obedience to these precepts—to which their intuition responds although they may not understand the method of their working—they may effect in the doing that which also may be effected by distinct and deliberate knowledge. So devotion and obedience to a Teacher may work towards liberation as knowledge might otherwise do.

Applying these principles in every direction the student will begin to realize how man is handicapped by ignorance, and how great is the part played by knowledge in human evolution. Men drift because they do not know; they are helpless because they are blind; the man who would finish his course more rapidly than will the common mass of men, who would leave the slothful crowd behind " as the racer leaves the hack ", he needs wisdom as well as love, knowledge as well as devotion. There is no need for him to wear out slowly the links of chains forged long ago; he can file them swiftly through, and be rid of them as effectively as though they slowly rusted away to set him free. The Ceasing of Karma

Karma brings us ever back to rebirth, binds us to the wheel of births and deaths. Good karma drags us back as relentlessly as bad, and the chain which is wrought out of our virtues holds as firmly and as closely as that forged from our vices. How then shall the weaving of the chain be put an end to, since man must think and feel as long as he lives, and thoughts and feelings are ever generating karma? The answer to this is the great lesson of the Bhagavad Gita, the lesson taught to the warrior prince. Neither to hermit nor to student was that lesson given, but to the warrior striving for victory, the prince immersed in the duties of his state.

Not in action but in desire, not in action but in attachment to its fruit, lies the binding force of action. An action is performed with desire to enjoy its fruit, a course is adopted with desire to obtain its results; the soul is expectant and Nature must reply to it, it has demanded and Nature must award. To every cause is bound its effect, to every action its fruit, and desire is the cord that links them together, the thread that runs between. If this could be burned up the connection would cease, and when all the bonds of the heart are broken the soul is free. Karma can then no longer hold it; karma can then no longer bind it; the wheel of cause and effect may continue to turn, but the soul has become the liberated Life.

Without attachment, constantly perform action which is duty, for performing action without attachment, man verily reacheth the Supreme.(Bhagavad Gita, iii, 19)

To perform this karma-yoga-—-yoga of action—as it is called, man must perform every action merely as duty, doing all in harmony with the Law. Seeking to conform to the Law on any plane of being on which he is busied, he aims at becoming a force working with the Divine Will for evolution, and yields a perfect obedience in every phase of his activity. Thus all his actions partake of the nature of sacrifice, and are offered for the turning of the Wheel of the Law, not for any fruit that they may bring; the action is performed as duty, the fruit is joyfully given for the helping of men; he has no concern with it, it belongs to the Law, and to the Law he leaves it for distribution.

And so we read:

Whose works are all free from the moulding of desire, whose actions are burned up by the fire of wisdom, he is called a Sage by the spiritually wise.

Having abandoned all attachment to the fruit of action, always content, seeking refuge in none, although doing actions, he, is not doing anything.

Free from desire, his thoughts controlled by the SELF, having abandoned all attachment, performing action by the body alone, he doth not commit sin.

Content with whatsoever he receiveth, free from the pairs of opposites, without envy, balanced in success and failure, though he hath acted he is not bound;

For with attachment dead, harmonious, his thoughts established in wisdom, his works, sacrifices, all his actions melt away. (Bhagavad Gita, iv, 19-23.)

Body and mind work out their full activities; with the body all bodily action is performed, with the mind all mental; but the SELF remains serene, untroubled, lending not of its eternal essence to forge the chains of time. Right action is never neglected, but is faithfully performed to the limit of the available power, renunciation of attachment to the fruit not implying any sloth or carelessness in acting:

As the ignorant act from attachment to action, O Bharata, so should the wise act without attachment, desiring the maintenance of mankind.

Let no wise man unsettle the mind of ignorant people attached to action: but acting in harmony (with Me) let him render all action attractive. (Bhagavad Gita, iii, 25-26)

The man who reaches this state of " inaction in action ", has learned the secret of the ceasing of karma: he destroys by knowledge the action he has generated in the past, he burns up the action of the present by devotion. Then it is that he attains the state spoken of by " John the divine " in Revelation, in which the man goeth no more out of the Temple. For the soul goes out of the Temple many and many a time into the plains of life, but the time arrives when he becomes a pillar, " a pillar in the Temple of my God "; that Temple is the universe of liberated souls, and only those who are bound to nothing for themselves can be bound to everyone in the name of the One Life.

These bonds of desire then, of personal desire, nay of individual desire, must be broken. We can see how the breaking will begin; and here conies in a mistake which many young students are apt to fall into, a mistake so natural and easy that it is constantly occurring. We do not break the " bonds of the heart" by trying to kill the heart. We do not break the bonds of desire by trying to turn ourselves into stones or pieces of metal unable to feel. The disciple becomes more sensitive, and not less so, as he nears his liberation, he becomes more tender and not more hard; for the perfect " disciple who is as the Master" is the one who answers to every thrill in the outside universe, who is touched by and responds to everything, who feels and answers to everything, who just because he desires nothing for himself is able to give everything to all. Such a one cannot be held by karma, he forges no bonds to bind the soul. As the disciple becomes more and more a channel of Divine Life to the world, he asks nothing save to be a channel, with wider and wider bed along which the great Life may flow: his only wish is that he may become a larger vessel, with less of obstacle in himself to hinder the outward pouring of the Life; working for nothing save to be of service, that is the life of discipleship, in which the bonds that bind are broken.

But there is one bond that breaks not ever, the bond of that real unity which is no bond, for it cannot be distinguished as separate, that which unites the One to the All, the disciple to the Master, the Master to his disciple; the Divine Life which draws us ever onwards and upwards, but binds us not to the wheel of birth and death. We are drawn back to earth—first by desire for what we enjoy there, then by higher and higher desires which still have earth for their region of fulfillment—for spiritual knowledge, spiritual growth, spiritual devotion. What is it, when all is accomplished, that still binds the Masters to the world of men? Not anything that the world can offer them. There is no knowledge on earth they have not; there is no power on earth that they wield not; there is no further experience that might enrich their lives; there is nothing that the world can give them, that can draw them back to birth. And yet they come, because a divine compulsion that is from within and from without sends them to the earth-—-which otherwise they might leave for ever—to help their brethren, to labour century after century, millennium after millennium, for the joy and service that make their love and peace ineffable with nothing that the earth can give them, save the joy of seeing other souls growing into their likeness, beginning to share with them the conscious life of God.

VII. Collective Karma

The gathering together of souls into groups, forming families, castes, nations, races, introduces a new element of perplexity into karmic results, and it is here that room is found for what are called " accidents " as well as for the adjustments continually being made by the Lords of Karma. It appears that while nothing can befall a man that is not " in his karma " as an individual, advantage may be taken of, say, a national or a seismic catastrophe to enable him to work off a piece of bad karma which would not normally have fallen into the life-span through which he is passing; it appears—I can only speak hereon speculatively, not having definite knowledge on this point—as though sudden death could not strike off a man's body unless he owed such a death to the Law, no matter into what whirl of catastrophic disaster he may be hurled; he would be what is called " miraculously preserved" amid the death and ruin that swept away his neighbours, and emerge unharmed from tempest or fiery outbreak. But if he owed a life, and were drawn by his national or family karma within the area of such a disturbance, then, although such sudden death had not been woven into his etheric double for that special life, no active interference might be made for his preservation; special care would be taken of him afterwards that he might not suffer unduly from his sudden snatching out of earth-life, but he would be allowed to pay his debt on the arising of such an opportunity, brought within his reach by the wider sweep of the Law, by the collective karma that involves him.

Similarly, benefits may accrue to him by this indirect action of the Law, as when he belongs to a nation that is enjoying the fruit of some good national karma; and he may thus receive some debt owed to him by Nature, the payment of which would not have fallen within his present lot had only his individual karma been concerned.

A man's birth in a particular nation is influenced by certain general principles of evolution as well as by his immediate characteristics. The soul in its slow development has not only to pass through the seven Root Races of a globe (I deal with the normal evolution of humanity), but also through the sub-races. This necessity imposes certain conditions, to which the individual karma must adapt itself, and a nation belonging to the sub-race through which the soul has to pass will offer the area within which the more special conditions needed must be found. Where long series of incarnations have been followed, it has been found that some individuals progress from sub-race to sub-race very regularly, whereas others are more erratic, taking repeated incarnations perhaps in one sub-race. Within the limits of the sub-race, the individual characteristics of the man will draw him towards one nation or another, and we may notice dominant national characteristics re-emerging on the stage of history en bloc after the normal interval of fifteen hundred years; thus crowds of Romans reincarnate as Englishmen, the enterprising, colonizing, conquering, imperial instincts reappearing as national attributes. A man in whom such national characteristics were strongly marked, and whose time for rebirth had come, would be drafted into the English nation by his karma and would then share the national destiny for good or for evil, so far as that destiny affected the fate of an individual.

The family tie is naturally of a more personal character than is the national, and those who weave bonds of close affection in one life tend to be drawn together again as members of the same family. Sometimes these ties recur very persistently life after life, and the destinies of two individuals are very intimately interwoven in successive incarnations. Sometimes, in consequence of the different lengths of the devachans necessitated by differences of intellectual and spiritual activity during the earth-lives spent together—members of a family may be scattered and may not meet again until after several incarnations. Speaking generally, the more close the tie in the higher regions of life, the greater the likelihood of rebirth in a family group. Here again the karma of the individual is affected by the inter-linked karmas of his family, and he may enjoy or suffer through these in a way not inherent in his own life-karma, and so receive or pay karmic debts, out-of-date, as we may say. So far as the personality is concerned, this seems to bring with it a certain balancing up or compensation in kama-loka and devachan, in order that complete justice may be done even to the fleeting personality.

The working out in detail of collective karma would carry us far beyond the limits of such an elementary work as the present and far beyond the knowledge of the writer; only these fragmentary hints can at present be offered to the student. For precise understanding a long study of individual cases would be necessary, traced through many thousands of years. Speculation on these matters is idle; it is patient observation that is needed.

There is, however, one other aspect of collective karma on which some word may fitly be said; the relation between men's thoughts and deeds and the aspects of external nature. On this obscure subject Mme. Blavatsky has the following:

Following Plato, Aristotle explained that the term

στοιχεῖα [elements] was understood only as meaning the incorporeal principles placed at each of the four great divisions of our cosmical world, to supervise them. Thus, no more than Christians do Pagans adore and worship the Elements and the (imaginary) cardinal points, but the " Gods " that respectively rule over them. For the Church, there are two kinds of Sidereal Beings, Angels and Devils. For the Kabalist and Occultist there is one class, and neither Occultist nor Kabalist makes any difference between the " Rectors of Light" and the " Rectores Tenebrarum," or Cosmocratores, whom the Roman Church imagines and discovers in the " Rectors of Light," as soon as any one of them is called by another name than the one she addresses him by. It is not the Rector, or Maharajah, who punishes or rewards, with or without " God's " permission or order, but man himself—his deeds, or Karma attracting individually and collectively (as in the case of whole nations sometimes) every kind of evil and calamity. We produce

84

Causes, and these awaken the corresponding powers in the Sidereal World, which are magnetically and irresistibly attracted to—and react upon—those who produce such causes; whether such persons are practically the evil-doers, or, simply " thinkers " who brood mischief. For thought is matter, we are taught by Modern Science; and "every particle of the existing matter must be a register of all that has happened," as Messrs. Jevons and Babbage in their Principles of Science tell the profane. Modern Science is every day drawn more into the maelstrom of Occultism: unconsciously no doubt, still very sensibly.

" Thought is matter ": not, of course, however, in the sense of the German Materialist Moleschott, who assures us that " thought is the movement of matter "—a statement of almost unparalleled absurdity. Mental states and bodily states are utterly contrasted as such. But that does not affect the position that every thought, in addition to its physical accompaniment (brain-change), exhibits an objective—though to us supersensuously objective—aspect on the astral plane. (The Secret Doctrine, i, 148, 149.)

It seems that when men generate a large number of malignant thought-forms of a destructive character, and when these congregate in huge masses on the astral plane, their energy may be, and is, precipitated on the physical plane, stirring up wars, revolutions, and social disturbances and upheavals of every kind, falling as collective karma on their progenitors and effecting widespread ruin. Thus then, collectively also man is the master of his destiny, and his world is moulded by his creative action.

Epidemics of crime and disease, cycles of accidents, have a similar explanation. Thought-forms of anger aid in the perpetration of a murder; these Elementals are nourished by the crime, and the results of the crime—the hatred and the revengeful thoughts of those who loved the victim, the fierce resentment of the criminal, his baffled fury when violently sent out of the world—still further reinforce their host with many malignant forms; these again from the astral plane impel an evil man to fresh crime, and again the circle of new impulses is trodden, and we have an epidemic of violent deeds. Diseases spread, and the thoughts of fear which follow their progress act directly as strengthened of the power of the disease; magnetic disturbances are set up and propagated, and react on the magnetic spheres of people within the affected area. In every direction, in endless fashions, do man's evil thoughts play havoc, as he who should have been a divine co-builder in the Universe uses his creative power to destroy.

Conclusion

Such is an outline of the great Law of Karma and of its workings, by a knowledge of which a man may accelerate his evolution, by the utilization of which a man may free himself from bondage, and become, long ere his race has trodden its course, one of the helpers and saviours of the world. A deep and steady conviction of the truth of this law gives to life an immovable serenity and a perfect fearlessness: nothing can touch us that we have not wrought, nothing can injure us that we have not merited. And as everything that we have sown must ripen into harvest in due season, and must be reaped, it is idle to lament over the reaping when it is painful; it may as well be done now as at any future time, since it cannot be evaded, and, once done, it cannot return to trouble us again. Painful karma may therefore well be faced with a joyful heart, as a thing to be gladly worked through and done with; it is better to have it behind us than before us, and every debt paid leaves us with less to pay. Would that the world knew and could feel the strength that comes from this resting on the Law! Unfortunately to most in the Western world it is a mere chimera, and even among Theosophists belief in karma is more an intellectual assent than a living and fruitful conviction in the light of which the life is lived. The strength of a belief, says Professor Bain, is measured by its influence on conduct, and belief in karma ought to make the life pure, strong, serene and glad. Only our own deeds can hinder us; only our own will can fetter us. Once let men recognize this truth, and the hour of their liberation has struck. Nature cannot enslave the soul that by wisdom has gained power, and uses both in love.

BOOK THREE
A STUDY IN KARMA

KARMA

(From The Light of Asia by Sir Edwin Arnold)
It knows not wrath nor pardon; utter true
Its measures mete, its faultless balance weighs;
Times are as nought, tomorrow it will judge,
 Or after many days.
By this the slayer's knife did stab himself;
The unjust judge hath lost his own defender;
The false tongue dooms its lie; the creeping thief
And spoiler rob, to render.
Such is the Law which moves to righteousness,
Which none at last can turn aside or stay;
The heart of it is Love, the end of it
Is Peace and Consummation sweet. Obey!

AMONG the many illuminating gifts to the western world, conveyed to it by the medium of the Theosophical Society, that of the knowledge of karma comes, perhaps, next in importance to that of reincarnation. It removes human thought and desire from the region of arbitrary happenings to the realm of law, and thus places man's future under his own control in proportion to the amount of his knowledge. The main conception of karma: "As a man soweth, so shall he also reap," is easy to grasp. But the application of this to daily life in detail, the method of its working and its far-reaching consequences – these are the difficulties which become more bewildering to the student as his knowledge increases. The principles on which any natural science is based are, for the most part, readily intelligible to people of fair intelligence and ordinary education; but as the student passes from principles to practice, from outline to details, he discovers that difficulties press upon him, and if he would wholly master his subject he finds himself compelled to become a specialist, and to devote long periods to the unraveling of the tangles which confront him. So is it also with this science of karma; the student cannot remain always in the domain of generalities; he must study the subdivisions of the primary law, must seek to apply it in all the circumstances of life, must learn how far it binds and how freedom becomes possible. He must learn to see in karma a universal law of nature, and learn also, as in face of nature as a whole, that conquest of and rule over her can only be gained by obedience.("Nature is conquered by obedience".)

I. FUNDAMENTAL PRINCIPLES

In order to understand karma, the student must begin with a clear view of certain fundamental principles, from the lack of which many remain constantly bewildered, asking endless questions which cannot find full solution without the solid laying of this basis. Therefore, in this study, I begin with these, though many of my readers will be already familiar with them, through previous statements of others and of myself. The fundamental conception, on which all later right thinking on karma rests, is that it is law – law eternal, changeless, invariable, inviolable, law which can never be broken, existing in the nature of things, informed Theosophists say: "You must not interfere with his karma." But whenever a natural law is working, you may interfere with it just so far as you can. You do not hear a person say solemnly: "You must not interfere with the law of gravitation." It is understood that gravitation is one of the conditions with which one has to reckon, and that one is perfectly at liberty to counteract any inconvenience it may cause by setting another force against it, by building a buttress to support that which otherwise would fall to the ground under the action of gravitation, or in any other way. When a condition in nature incommodes us, we use our intelligence to circumvent it, and no one ever dreams of telling us that we must not "interfere with" or change any condition which we dislike. We can only interfere when we have knowledge, for we cannot annihilate any natural force, nor prevent it from acting. But we can neutralize, we can turn aside, its action if we have at command another sufficient force, and while I will never abate for us one jot of its activity, it can be held up, opposed, circumvented, exactly according to our knowledge of its nature and working, and the forces at our disposal. Karma is no more "sacred" than any other natural law; all laws of nature are expressions of the divine nature, and we live and move within them; but they are not mandatory; they are forces which set up conditions amid which we live, and which work in us as well as outside of us; we can manipulate them; we understand them, and as our intelligence unfolds we become more and more their masters, until the man becomes superman, and material nature becomes his servant.

II. LAWS: NATURAL AND MAN-MADE

Much confusion has arisen in this matter, because, in the West, "natural" laws have been regarded as apart from mental and moral laws, whereas mental and moral laws are as much part of natural law as the laws of electricity, and all laws are part of the order of nature. Natural law has been, in many minds, confused with human law, and the arbitrariness of human legislation has been imported into the realm of natural law. Laws affecting physical phenomena have been rescued from this arbitrariness by science, but the mental and moral worlds are still in the chaos of lawlessness. Not a divine command, but the immanence of the divine nature, conditions our existence, and where prophets have laid down moral laws, these have been declarations of inevitable sequences in the moral world, known to the prophet, unknown to his ignorant hearers; because of their ignorance, his hearers have regarded his declarations as arbitrary commands of a divine lawgiver, sent through him, instead of as mere statements of fact concerning the succession of moral phenomena in a region as orderly as the physical. Law, in the secondary social sense, is an enactment laid down by an authority regarded as legitimate. It may be the edict of an autocrat, or the act of a legislative assembly; in either case the force of the law depends on the recognition of the authority which makes it. Among the Hindus we find the ideas both of man-made and natural law. The King, in the conception of the Manu, is an autocrat, and the subject must obey; but above the King is a Law to which he in his turn must be obedient, a Law which acts automatically and is in the nature of things. In spite of his autocracy, he is bound by the supreme Law, which will crush him if he disregards it. Weakness oppressed is said to be the most fatal enemy of Kings; the tears of the weak sap the foundation of thrones, and the suffering of the nation destroys the ruler. The physical and the super-physical worlds interpenetrate each other, and causes set going in the one bring about results in the other.

The King and his Council in ancient India made the laws of the State, but these were artificial, not natural, laws; they were binding on the subjects, and were enforced by penalties, but such laws differ wholly from natural law. It seems a pity that one word should be used for two things so different as natural and artificial laws, yet they are clearly distinguishable by their characteristics. Artificial laws are changeable; those who make them can alter them or repeal them. Natural laws are unchanging; they cannot be altered nor repealed, but lie in the nature of things. Artificial laws are local, while natural are universal. The law in any country against robbery may be enforced by any penalty chosen by the legislator; sometimes the hand is cut off, sometimes the thief is sent to goal, sometimes he is hanged. Moreover, the infliction of the penalty is dependent on the discovery of the crime. A penalty which is variable and artificial, and which may be escaped, is obviously not causally related to the crime it punishes. A natural law has no penalty, but one condition follows invariably on another; if a man steals, his nature becomes more thievish, the tendency to dishonesty is increased, and the difficulty of being honest becomes greater; this consequence works in every case, in all countries; and the knowledge or ignorance of others as to theft makes no difference in the consequence. A penalty which is local, variable and escapable is a sign that the law is artificial, and not natural. A natural law is a sequence of conditions; such a condition being present, such another condition will invariably fellow. If you want to bring about condition No.2, you must find or make condition No.1, and then condition No.2 will follow as an invariable consequence. These sequences never vary when left to themselves, but if a new condition is introduced the succeeding condition will be altered. Thus water runs down a slanting channel in accordance with the force of gravitation, and if you pour water in at the top, it will invariably run down the slope; but you can obstruct the flow by putting an obstacle in the way, and then the resistance which the obstacle opposes to the force of gravitation balances it, but the force of gravitation remains active and is found in the pressure on the obstacle. The first condition is called the cause, the resulting condition the effect, and the same cause always brings about the same effect, provided no other cause is introduced; in the latter case, the effect is the resultant of both.

III. THE LAW OF LAWS

Karma is natural law in the full sense of the term; it is Universal Causation, the Law of Cause and Effect. It may be said to underlie all special laws, all causes and effects. It is natural law in all its aspects and in all its subdivisions; it is not a special law, but a universal condition, the one law whereon all other laws depend, of which all other laws are partial expressions. The Bhagavad-Gita says that none who are embodied can escape it – Shining Ones, human beings, animals, vegetables, minerals, are all evolving within this universal law; even the LOGOS Himself, embodied in a universe, comes within a larger sweep of this law of all manifestation. So long as any one is related to matter, embodied in matter, so long is he within karmic law. A being may escape from or transcend one or other of its aspects, but he cannot, while remaining in manifestation, go outside this law.

IV. THE ETERNAL NOW

This universal Law of Causation binds together into one all that happens within a manifestation, for it is universal interrelation. Interrelation between all that exists – that is karma. It is therefore coexistent, simultaneous, with the coming into existence of any special universe. Therefore karma is eternal as the Universal Self. The interrelation of everything always is. It never begins; it never ceases to be. "The unreal has no being; the real never ceases to be." Nothing exists isolated, alone, out of relation, and karma is the interrelation of all that exists. It is manifest during the manifestation of a universe, as regards that universe; it becomes latent in its dissolution.

In the All everything IS always; all that has been, all that now is manifest, all that will be, all that can be, all possibilities as well as all actualities, are ever in being in the All. That which is outwards, the forth-going, existence, the unfolded, is the manifested universe. That which IS as really, although inwards, the infolded, is the unmanifested universe. But the Within, the Unmanifested, is as real as the Without, the Manifested. The interrelation between beings, in or out of manifestation, is the eternal karma. As Being never ceases, so karma never ceases, but always is. When part of that which is simultaneous in the All becomes manifested as a universe, the eternal interrelation becomes successive, and is seen as cause and effect. In the one Being, the All, everything is linked to everything else, everything is related to everything else, and in the phenomenal, the manifested universe, these links and relations are drawn out into successive happenings, causally connected in the order of their succession in time, i.e., in appearance.

Some students shrink from a metaphysical view such as this, but unless this idea of eternal Being, within which all beings ever are, is grasped, the centre cannot be reached. So long as we think from the circumference, there is always a question behind every answer, endless beginnings and endings with a "Why?" behind each beginning. If the student would escape this, he must patiently seek the centre, and let the concept of All sink into his mind, until it becomes an ever-present part of his mental equipment, and then the universes on the circumference become intelligible, and the universal interrelation between all things, seen from the simultaneity of the centre, naturally becomes cause and effect in the successions on the circumference. It has been said that the Eternal (The Hindu name is Brahman, or more strictly, Nirguna Brahman, the Brahman without attributes) is an ocean, which throws up universes as waves. The ocean symbolises being without form, ever the same. The wave, by virtue of being a part, has form and attributes. The waves rise and fall; they break into foam, and the spray of the waves is as worlds in a universe.

Or we may think of a huge waterfall, like Niagara, where the mass of its torrent is one ere it falls, and then it divides into innumerable drops, which separately reflect the light; and the drops are as worlds, and the rainbow they make is the many-coloured life. But the water is one while the drops are many, and life is one though beings are many. God manifest or unmanifest is one and the same, though different, though showing attributes in manifestation, and attributes in un-manifestation; the LOGOS and His universe are one, though He is the unity and the universe the diversity, He is the life and the universe the forms. Out of manifestation karma is latent, for the beings of the manifested are but concepts in the unmanifested; in manifestation karma is active, for all the parts of a world, of a system, of a universe, are inter-related. Science declares that no movement of a part can take place without affecting the whole, and scientifically all are agreed. The inter-relations are universal, and none can be broken, for the breaking of one would break the unity of the whole. The inviolability of natural law rests on its universality, and a breach of law in any part would mean universal chaos.

V. SUCCESSION

We have seen that as the manifestation of a universe implies succession of phenomena, so the universal inter-relation becomes the sequence of cause and effect. But each effect becomes in turn a cause, and so on endlessly, the difference between cause and effect not being one of nature but of relation. The inter-relations which exist in the thought of the Eternal become the inter-relations between phenomena in the manifested universe – the portion of the thought put forth as a universe. Before the manifestation of any special universe, there will be, in the Eternal, the thought of the universe which is to be, and its inter-relations. That which exists simultaneously out of time and space in the Eternal Now, gradually appears in time and space as successive phenomena. The moment you conceive a universe as made up of phenomena, you are obliged to think of these phenomena successively, one after another; but in the thought of the Eternal they always are, and the limitation of succession has there no existence.

Even in the lower worlds, where the measures of time are so different from each other, we catch a glimpse of the increasing limitations of denser matter. Mozart tells us of a state of consciousness in which he received a musical composition as a single impression, although in his waking consciousness he could only reproduce that single impression in a succession of notes. Or again, we may look at a picture, and receive a single mental impression – a landscape, a battle; but an ant, crawling over that picture, would see no whole, only successive impressions from the parts travelled over.

By simile, by analogy, we may gain some idea of the difference of a universe as it appears to the LOGOS and as it appears to us. To Him, a single impression, a perfect whole; to us an immense sequence, slowly unfolding. So what is to Him inter-relation becomes to us succession. Instead of seeing childhood, youth, old age as a whole, we see them successively, day by day, year by year. That which is simultaneous and universal becomes successive and particular to our small minds, crawling over the world as the ant over the picture.

Go up a mountain and look down on a town, and you can see how the houses are related to each other in blocks, streets, and so on. You realise them as a whole. But when you go down into the town you must pass from street to street, seeing each separately, successively. So in karma, we see the relations only one by one, and one after another, not even realising the successive relations, so limited is our view.

Such similes may often help us to grasp the invisible things, and may act as crutches to our halting imagination. And out of all this we lay our foundation stone for our study of karma.

Karma is universal inter-relation, and is seen in any universe as the Law of Causation, in consequence of the successive appearance of phenomena in the becoming, or coming forth, of the universe.

VI. CAUSATION

The idea of causation has been challenged in modern times, Huxley, for instance, contending, in the Contemporary Review, that we only knew sequence, not causation; he said that if a ball moved after it was hit by a bat, you should not say that the blow of the bat caused the movement, but only that it was followed by the movement. This extreme scepticism came out strongly in some of the great men of the nineteenth century, a reaction from the ready credulity and many unproved assumptions of the Middle Ages. The reaction had its use, but is now gradually passing away, as extremes ever do.

The idea of causation arises naturally in the human mind, though unprovable by the senses; when a phenomenon has been invariably followed by another phenomenon for long periods of time, the two become linked together in our minds, and when one appears, the mind, by association of ideas, expects the second; thus the fact that night has been followed by day from time immemorial gives us a firm conviction that the sun will rise tomorrow as on countless yesterdays. Succession alone, however, does not necessarily imply causation; we do not regard day as the cause of night, nor night as the cause of day, because they invariably succeed each other. To assert causation, we need more than invariable succession; we need that the reason shall see that which the senses are unable to discern – a relation between the two things which brings about the appearance of the second when the first appears. The succession of day and night is not caused by either; both are caused by the relation of the earth to the sun; that relation is a true cause, recognised as such by the reason, and as long as the relation exists unchanged, day and night will be its effect. In order to see one thing as the cause of another, the reason must establish a relation between them which is sufficient for the production of one by the other; then, and then only, can we rightly assert causation. The links between phenomena that are never broken, and that are recognised by the reason as an active relation, bringing into manifestation the second phenomenon whenever the first is manifested, we call causation. They are the shadows of inter-relations existing in the Eternal, outside space and time, and they extend over the life of a universe, wherever the conditions exist for their manifestation. Causation is an expression of the nature of the LOGOS, an Emanation of the eternal Reality; wherever there is interrelation in the Eternal which demands succession for its manifestation in time, there is causation.

VII. THE LAWS OF NATURE

Our next step in our study is a consideration of the "Laws of Nature". The whole universe is included within the ideas of succession and causation, but when we come to what we call the laws of nature, we are unable to say over what area they extend. Scientists find themselves compelled to speak with greater and greater caution as they travel beyond the limit of actual observation. Causes and effects which are continuous within the area of our observation may not exist in other regions, or workings which are here observed as invariable may be interrupted by the irruption of some cause outside the "known" of our time, though probably not outside the knowable. Between 1850 and 1890 there were many positive statements as to the conservation of energy and the indestructibility of matter. It was said that there existed in the universe a certain amount of energy, incapable of diminution or of increase; that all forces were forms of that energy, that the amount of any given force, as heat, might vary, but not the total amount of energy. As 20 may be made up of 20 units, or of 10 twos, or of 5 fours, or of 12+8,) and so on, but the total remains as 20, so with the varying forms and the total amount. With regard to matter, again, similar statements were made; it was indestructible, and hence remained ever the same in amount; some, like Ludwig Buchner, declared that the chemical elements were indestructible, that "an atom of carbon was ever an atom of carbon," and so on.

On these two ideas science was built up, and they formed the basis of materialism. But now it is realised that chemical elements are dissoluble, and that the atom itself may be a swirl in the ether, or perhaps a mere hole where ether is not. There may be atoms through which force pours in, others through which it pours out – whence? – whither? May not physical matter become intangible, resolve itself into ether? May not ether give birth to new matter? All is doubtful where once certainty reigned. Yet has a universe its "Ring-Pass-Not". Within a given area only can we speak with certainty of a "law of nature".

What is a law of nature? Mr. J.N. Farquhar, in the Contemporary Review for July, 1910, in an article on Hinduism, declares that if Hindus want to carry out reforms, they must abandon the idea of karma. As well might he say that if a man wants to fly he must abandon the idea of an atmosphere. To understand the law of karma is not to renounce activity, but to know the conditions under which activity is best carried on. Mr. Farquhar, who has evidently studied modern Hinduism carefully, has not grasped the idea of karma as taught in ancient scripture and in modern science.

A law of nature is not a command, but a statement of conditions. This cannot be repeated too often, nor insisted on too strongly. Nature does not order this thing or the other; she says: "Here are certain conditions; where these exist, such and such a result will invariably follow." A law of nature is an invariable sequence. If you do not like the result, change the preceding conditions. Ignorant, you are helpless, at the mercy of nature's hurtling forces; wise, you are master, and her forces serve you obediently. Every law of nature is an enabling, not a compelling, force, but knowledge is necessary for utilising her powers.

Water boils at 100 degrees C. under normal pressure. This is the condition. You go up a mountain; pressure diminishes; water boils at 95 degrees. Now water at 95 degrees will not make good tea. Does Nature then forbid you to have good tea on a mountain-top? Not at all: under normal pressure water boils at the necessary temperature for tea-making; you have lost pressure; supply the deficit; imprison your escaping steam till it adds the necessary pressure, and you can make your tea with water at 100 degrees. If you want to produce water by the union of hydrogen and oxygen, you require a certain temperature, and can obtain it from the electric spark. If you insist on keeping the temperature at zero, or in substituting nitrogen for hydrogen, you cannot have water. Nature lays down the conditions which result in the production of water, and you cannot change them; she neither supplies nor withholds water; you are free to have it or to go without it; if you want it, you must bring together the necessary things and thus make the conditions. Without these, no water. With these, inevitably water. Are you bound or free? Free as to making the conditions; bound as to the result, when once you have made them. Knowing this, the scientific man, face to face with a difficulty, does not sit down helplessly; he finds out the conditions under which he can bring about a result, learns how to make the conditions, sure that he can rely on the result.

VIII. A LESSON OF THE LAW

This is the great lesson taught by science to the present generation. Religion has taught it for ages, but dogmatically rather than rationally. Science proves that knowledge is the condition of freedom, and that only as man knows can he compel. The scientific man observes sequences; over and over again he performs his testing experiments; he eliminates all that is casual, collateral, irrelevant, and slowly, surely, discovers what constitutes an invariable causative sequence. Once sure of his facts, he acts with indubitable assurance, and nature, without shadow of turning, rewards his rational certainty with success.

Out of this assurance grows "the sublime patience of the investigator". Luther Burbank, in California, will sow millions of seeds, select some thousands of plants, pair a few hundreds, and patiently march to his end; he can trust the laws of nature, and, if he fails, he knows that the error lies with him, not with them.

There is a law of nature that masses of matter tend to move towards the earth. Shall I then say: "I cannot walk up the stairs; I cannot fly in the air"? Nay, there are other laws. I pit against the force that holds me on the ground, another force stored in my muscles, and I raise my body by means of it. A person with muscles weak from fever may have to stay on the ground-floor, helpless; but I break no law when I put forth muscular force, and walk upstairs.

The inviolability of Law does not bind – it frees. It makes Science possible, and rationalises human effort. In a lawless universe, effort would be futile, reasons would be useless. We should be savages, trembling in the grip of forces, strange, incalculable, terrible. Imagine a chemist in a laboratory where nitrogen was now inert, now explosive, where oxygen vivified today and stifled tomorrow! In a lawless universe we should not dare to move, not knowing what any action might bring about. We move sagely, surely, because of the inviolability of Law.

IX. KARMA DOES NOT CRUSH

Now Karma is the great law of nature, with all that that implies. As we are able to move in the physical universe with security, knowing its laws, so may we move in the mental and moral universes with security also, as we learn their laws. The majority of people, with regard to their mental and moral defects, are much in the position of a man who should decline to walk upstairs because of the law of gravitation. They sit down helplessly, and say: "That is my nature. I cannot help it." True, it is the man's nature, as he has made it in the past, and it is "his karma". But by a knowledge of karma he can change his nature, making it other tomorrow than it is today. He is not in the grip of an inevitable destiny, imposed upon him from outside; he is in a world of law, full of natural forces which he can utilise to bring about the state of things which he desires. Knowledge and will – that is what he needs. He must realize that karma is not a power which crushes, but a statement of conditions out of which invariable results accrue. So long as he lives carelessly, in a happy-go-lucky way, so long will he be like a man floating on a stream, stuck by any passing log, blown aside by any casual breeze, caught in any chance eddy. This spells failure, misfortune, unhappiness. The law enables him to compass his ends successfully, and places within his reach forces which he can utilise. He can modify, change, remake on other lines the nature which is the inevitable outcome of his previous desires, thoughts, and actions; that future nature is as inevitable as the present, the result of the conditions which he now deliberately makes. "Habit is second nature," says the proverb, and thought creates habits. Where there is Law, no achievement is impossible, and karma is the guarantee of man's evolution into mental and moral perfection.

X. APPLY THIS LAW

We have now to apply this law to ordinary human life, to apply principle to practice. It has been the loss of the intelligible relations between eternal principles and transitory events that has rendered modern religion so inoperative in common life. A man will clean up his backyard when he understands the relation between dirt and disease; but he leaves his mental and moral backyards uncleansed, because he sees no relation between his mental and moral defects and the various ghastly after-death experiences with which he is threatened by religions. Hence he either disbelieves the threats and goes carelessly on his way, or hopes to escape consequences by some artificial compact with the authorities. In either case, he does not cleanse his ways. When he realizes that law is as inviolable in the mental and moral worlds as in the physical, it may well be hoped that he will become as reasonable in the former as he already is in the latter.

XI. MAN IN THE THREE WORLDS

Man, as we know, is living normally in three worlds, the physical, emotional and mental, is put into contact with each by a body formed of its type of matter, and acts in each through the appropriate body. He therefore creates results in each according to their respective laws and powers, and all these come within the all-embracing law of karma. During his daily life in waking consciousness he is creating "karma," i.e. results, in these three worlds, by action, desire and thought. While his physical body is asleep, he is creating karma in two worlds – the emotional and the mental, the amount of karma then created by him depending on the stage he has reached in evolution.

We may confine ourselves to these three worlds, for those above them are not inhabited consciously by the average man; but we should, none the less, remember that we are like trees, the roots of which are fixed in the higher worlds, and their branches spread in the three lower worlds in which dwell our mortal bodies, and in which our consciousnesses are working.

Laws work within their own worlds, and must be studied as though their workings were independent; just as every science studies the laws working within its own department, but does not forget the wider working of further-reaching conditions, so must man, while working in the three departments, physical, emotional and mental, remember the sweep of law which includes them all within its area of activity. In all departments laws are inviolable and unchangeable, and each brings about its own full effect, although the final result of their interaction is the effective force that remains when all balancing of opposing forces has been made. All that is true of laws in general is true of karma, the great law. Causes being present, events must follow. But by taking away, or adding causes, events must be modified.

A person gets drunk; may he say: "My karma is to get drunk"? He gets drunk because of certain tendencies existing in himself, the presence of loose companions, and an environment where drink is sold. Let us suppose that he wishes to conquer his evil habit; he knows the three conditions that lead him into drunkenness. He may say: "I am not strong enough to resist my own tendencies in the presence of drink and the company of loose-livers. I will not go where there is drink, nor will I associate with men who tempt me to drink." He changes the conditions, eliminating two of them, though unable immediately to change the third, and the new result is that he does not get drunk. He is not "interfering with karma," but is relying on it; nor is a friend "interfering with karma," if he persuades him to keep away from boon companions. There is no karmic command to a man to get drunk, but only the existence of certain conditions in the midst of which he certainly will get drunk; there is, it is true, another way of changing the conditions, the putting forth a strong effort of will; this also introduces a new condition, which will change the result – by addition instead of elimination.

In the only sense in which a man can "interfere" with the laws of nature he is perfectly at liberty to do so, as much as he likes and can. He can inhibit the acting of one force by bringing another against it; he can overcome gravitation by muscular effort. In this sense, he may interfere with karma as much as he likes, and should interfere with it when the results are objectionable. But the expression is not a happy one, and it is liable to be misunderstood.

The law is: such and such causes bring about such and such results. The law is unchangeable, but the play of phenomena is ever-changing. The mightiest cause of all causes is human will and human reason, and yet this is the cause which is, for the most part, omitted when people talk of karma. We are causes, because we are the divine will, one with God in our essential being, although hampered by ignorance and working through gross matter, which impedes us until we conquer, by spiritualising, it. The changelessness of karma is not the changelessness of effects but of law, and it is this which makes us free. Truly slaves should we be in a world in which everything went by chance. But according to our knowledge are our freedom and our safety in a world of law. In the Middle Ages, chemists were by no means free to bring about the results they desired, but they had to accept results as they came, unforeseen and for the most part undesired, even to their own serious injury. The result of an experiment might be a useful product, or it might be the reduction of the experimenter into fragments. Roger Bacon set going causes which cost him an eye and a finger, and occasionally stretched him senseless on the floor of his cell; outside our knowledge we are in peril, and any cause we set going may wreck us, for we are mostly Roger Bacons in the mental and moral worlds; inside our knowledge we may move with freedom and safety, as the well-trained chemist moves today. It is true in all the three worlds in which we live, that the more we know, the more can we foresee and control. Because law is inviolable and changeless, therefore knowledge is the condition of freedom. Let us then study karma, and apply our knowledge to the guidance of our lives. So many people say: "Oh! how I wish I were good," and do not use the law to create the causes which result in goodness; as though a chemist should say: "Oh! how I wish I had water," without making the conditions which would produce it.

Again, we must remember that each force works along its own particular line, and that when a number of forces impinge on a particular point, the resultant force is the outcome of all of them. As in our school days we learned how to construct a parallelogram of forces and thus find the resultant of their composition; so with karma may we learn to understand the conflict of forces and their composition to yield a single resultant. We hear people asking why a good man fails in business while a bad man succeeds. But there is no causal connection between goodness and money-getting. We might at well say: "I am a very good man; why cannot I fly in the air?" Goodness is not a cause of flying, nor does it bring in money. Tennyson touched on a great law when, in his poem on "Wages," he declared that the wages of virtue were not "dust," nor rest, nor pleasure, but the glory of an active immortality. "Virtue is its own reward" in the fullest sense of the words. If we are truthful, our reward is that our nature becomes more truthful, and so sequentially with every virtue. Karmic results can only be of the nature of their causes; they are not arbitrary, like human rewards.

XII. UNDERSTAND THE TRUTH

This seems to be obvious: whence then arises the general instinct that success in life should accompany goodness? We can successfully combat an error only when we understand the truth which lies at the heart of it, gives it its vitality, and leads to its spread and its persistence. The truth in this case is that, if a man puts himself into accord with the divine law, happiness is the result of such harmony. The error is to identify worldly success with happiness, and to disregard the element of time. A man going into business determines to be truthful, and to take no unfair advantage over others. He sees those who are untruthful and unscrupulous going ahead of him; if he is weak, he becomes discouraged, even, perchance, imitates them. If he is strong, he says: "I will work in harmony with the divine law, no matter what may be the immediate worldly results": inner peace and happiness are then his, but success does not accrue to him; nevertheless, in the long run even that may fall to him, for what he loses in money he gains in confidence, whereas the man who once betrays may at any time betray again, and none will trust him. In a competitive society, lack of scrupulousness yields immediate success, whereas in a cooperative society conscientiousness would "pay". To give starvation wages to workers forced by competition to accept them may lead to immediate success as against business rivals, and the man who gives a decent living wage may find himself outpaced in the race for wealth; but, in the long run, the latter will have better work done for him, and in the future will reap the harvest of happiness whereof he sowed the seed. We must decide on our course and accept its results, not looking for money as payment for goodness, nor seeing injustice when unscrupulous shrewdness reaches that at which it aimed.

An instructive, if not very pleasant, Indian story is told of a man who wronged another, and the injured man cried for redress to the King. When the punishment to be inflicted on his enemy was given into his hands, he prayed the King to enrich his foe; asked for the reason of his strange behaviour, he grimly said that wealth and worldly prosperity would give him greater opportunities for wrongdoing, and would thus entail on him bitter suffering in the life after death. Often the worst enemy of virtue is in easy material conditions, and these, which are spoken of as good karma, are often the reverse in their results. Many who do fairly well in adversity go astray in prosperity, and become intoxicated with worldly delights.

Let us now consider how a man affects his surroundings, or, in scientific phrase, how the organism acts on its environment.

XIII. MAN AND HIS SURROUNDINGS

Man affects his surroundings in innumerable ways, which may all be classified into three modes of self-expression: he affects them by Will, by Thought, by Action.

The developed man is able to draw his energies together and to fuse them into one, ready to go forth from him, and to cause action. This concentration of his energies into a single force, held in suspense within him, in leash ready for outrush, is Will; it is an interior concentration, one mode of the triple Self-expression. In the subhuman kingdoms, and in the lower divisions of the human, the pleasure-giving and pain-giving objects around the living creature draw out its energies, and we call these multifarious energies brought out by external objects its desires, whether of attraction or repulsion. Only when these are all drawn in, united and pointed towards a single aim, can we term this single energy, ready to go forth, the Will. This Will is Self-expression, i.e., it is directed by the Self; the Self determines the line to be taken, basing its determination on previous experience. In the subhuman and lower human kingdoms, desires are an important factor in karma, giving rise to most mixed results; in the higher human, Will is the most potent karmic cause, and as man transmutes desires into Will, he "rules his stars".

The mode of Self-expression called Thought belongs to the aspect of the Self by which he becomes aware of the outer world, the aspect of Cognition. This obtains knowledge, and the working of the Self on the knowledge obtained is Thought. This, again, is an important factor in karma, since it is creative, and as we know, builds character.

The mode of Self-expression which directly affects the environment, the energy giving forth from the Self, is Activity, the action of the Self on the Not-Self. The power of concentrating all energies into one is Will; the power of becoming aware of an external world is Cognition; the power of affecting that outside world is Activity. This action is inevitably followed by a reaction from the outside world – karma. The inner cause of the reaction is Will; the nature of the reaction is due to Cognition; the immediate provoker of the reaction is Activity. These spin the three threads of the karmic rope.

xiv. THE THREE FATES

"God created man in His own image," says a Hebrew Scripture, and the Trinities of the great religions are the symbols of the three aspects of the divine consciousness, reflected in the triplicity of the human. The first Logos of the Theosophist, the Mahadeva of the Hindu, the Father of the Christians, has Will as predominant, and shows forth the power of sovereignty, the Law by which the universe is built. The Second Logos, Vishnu, the Son, is Wisdom, that all-sustaining and all-pervading power by which the universe is preserved. The Third Logos, Brahma, the Holy Spirit, is the Agent, the creative power by which the universe is brought into manifestation. There is nothing in divine or human consciousness which does not find itself within one or other of these modes of Self-expression.

Again, matter has three fundamental qualities responsive severally to these modes of consciousness, and without these it could no more be manifested than Consciousness could express itself without its modes. It has inertia (tamas), the very foundation of all, the stability necessary to existence, the quality which answers to Will. It has mobility (rajas), the capacity to be moved, answering to Activity. It has rhythm (sattva), the equaliser of movement (without which movement would be chaotic, destructive), answering to Cognition. The Yoga system, considering all from the standpoint of consciousness, names this rhythmic quality "cognisability," that which makes that matter should be known by Spirit.

All that is in our consciousness, affecting the environment, and all the environment affected by our consciousness, make up our world. The interrelation between our consciousness and our environment is our karma. By these three modes of consciousness we spin our individual karma, the universal interrelation between Self and Not-Self being specialized by us into this individual interrelation As we rise above separateness, the individual again becomes the universal interrelation, but this universal interrelation cannot be transcended while manifestation endures. This specializing of the universal, and the later universalizing of the special make up of the "world's eternal ways" – the Path of Forthgoing to gather experience, the Path of Return, bringing the sheaves of experience home; this is the Great Wheel of Evolution, so relentless when seen from the standpoint of Matter, so beauteous when seen from the standpoint of Spirit.

"Life is not a cry, but a song."

xv. THE PAIR OF TRIPLETS

Thus we have three factors in spirit for the creation of Karma, and three corresponding qualities in matter, and we must study these in order to make our Karma that which we would have it be. We may study them in any order, but for many reasons it is convenient to take the cognitive factor first, because in that lies the power of knowledge and of choice. We can change our desires by the use of thought, we cannot change our thoughts, though we may colour them, by desire; so, in the final analysis action is set in motion by thought.

In the earliest stages of savagery as with the newly born infant action is caused by attractions and repulsions. But almost immediately memory comes in, the memory of an attraction, with the wish to re-experience it; the memory of a repulsion, with the wish to avoid it. A thing has given pleasure, it is remembered, i.e., thought about, it is desired, action to grasp it follows. The three cannot really be separated, for there is no action which is not preceded by thought and desire, and which does not again set them going, after it is performed. Action is the outer sign of the invisible thought and desire, and in its very accomplishment gives birth to a fresh thought and desire. The three form a circle, perpetually retraced.

xvi. THOUGHT, THE BUILDER

Now thought works on matter; every change in consciousness is answered by a vibration in matter, and a similar change, however often repeated, brings about a similar vibration. This vibration is strongest in the matter nearest to you, and the matter nearest to you is your own mental body. If you repeat a thought, it repeats the corresponding vibration, and, as when matter has vibrated in a particular way once it is easier for it to vibrate in that same way again than to vibrate in a new way, the more often you repeat a thought the more ready the vibrationary response. Presently, after much repetition, a tendency will be set up in the matter of your mental body, automatically to repeat the vibration on its own account; when it does this – since the vibration in matter and the thought in consciousness are inseparably linked – the thought appears in the mind without any previous activity on the part of consciousness.

Hence when you have thought over a thing – a virtue, an emotion, a wish – and have deliberately come to the conclusion that it is a desirable thing to have that virtue, to feel that emotion, to be moved by that wish, you quietly set to work to create a habit of thought.

You think deliberately of it every morning for a few minutes, and soon you find that it arises spontaneously in the mind (by the aforesaid automatic activity of matter). You persist in your thought-creation until you have formed a strong habit of thought, a habit which can only be changed by an equally prolonged process of thinking in the opposite direction. Even against the opposition of the will, the thought recurs to the mind – as many have found when they are unable to sleep in consequence of the involuntary recurrence of a harassing thought. If you have thus established the habit, say, of honesty, you will act honestly automatically; and if some strong gust of desire sweeps you into dishonesty on some occasion, the honest habit will torment you as it would never torment a habitual thief. You have created the habit of honesty; the thief has no such habit; hence you suffer mentally when the habit is broken, and the thief suffers not at all. Persistence in strengthening such a mental habit until it is stronger than any force which can be brought to bear upon it makes the reliable man; he literally cannot lie, cannot steal; he has built himself an impregnable virtue.

By thought, then, you can build any habit you choose to build. There is no virtue which you cannot create by thought. The forces of nature work with you, for you understand how to use them, and they become your servants.

If you love your husband, your wife, your child, you find that this emotion of love causes happiness in those who feel it. If you spread the love outwards to others, an increase of happiness results. You, seeing this and wishful for the happiness of all, deliberately begin to think love to others, in an ever wider and wider circle, until the love-attitude is your normal attitude towards all you meet. You have created the love-habit, and have generalized an emotion into a virtue, for a virtue is only a good emotion made general and permanent (See Bhagavan Das' The Science of Emotions)

Everything is under law; you cannot obtain mental ability or moral virtue by sitting still and doing nothing. You can obtain both by strenuous and persevering thinking. You can build your mental and moral nature by thinking, for "man is created by thought; what he thinks upon, that he becomes; therefore think" on that which you aspire to be, and inevitably it shall be yours. Thus shall you become a mental and moral athlete, and your character shall grow rapidly; you made in the past the character with which you were born; you are making now the character with which you will die, and will return. This is karma. Every one is born with a character, and the character is the most important part of karma. The Musalman says that "a man is born with his destiny tied round his neck". For a man's destiny depends chiefly on his character. A strong character can overcome the most unfavourable circumstances, and overclimb the most difficult obstacles. A weak character is buffeted by circumstances, and fails before the most trivial obstacles.

xvii. PRACTICAL MEDITATION

The whole theory of meditation is built upon these laws of thought; for meditation is only deliberate and persevering thought, aimed at a specific object, and hence is a potent karmic cause. By using knowledge and thought to modify character, you can bring about very quickly a desired result. If you were born a coward, you can think yourself brave; if you were born dishonest, you can think yourself honest: if you were born untruthful, you can think yourself truthful. Have confidence in yourself and in the law. There is another point we must not forget. Concrete thought finds its natural realisation in action, and if you do not act out a thought, then by reaction you weaken the thought. Strenuous action along the line of the thinking must follow the thought, otherwise progress will be slow.

Realise, then, that while you cannot now help the character with which you were born, while it is a fact which must profoundly influence your present destiny, marking out your line of activity in this life, yet you can, by thought and by action based thereon, change your inborn character, eliminate its weaknesses, eradicate its faults, strengthen its good qualities, enlarge its capacities. You are born with a given character, but you can change it. Knowledge is offered to you as to the means of changing, and each must put that knowledge into practice for himself.

XVIII. WILL AND DESIRE

Desire and Activity remain to be considered. Will is the energy prompting to action, and while it is attracted and repelled by outside objects, we call it desire, the lower aspect of Will, as thought is the lower aspect of Cognition. If a man, confronted by a pleasure-giving object, grasps it without thought, he is moved by desire; if he holds himself back, saying: "I must not enjoy it now, because I have a duty to perform," he is moved by Will. When the energy of the Self is controlled and guided by right reason, it is Will: when it rushes out unbridled, drawn hither and thither by attractive objects, it is Desire.

Desire arises in us spontaneously; we like one thing, we dislike another, and our likes and dislikes are involuntary; are not under the control of the Will nor of the reason. We may make up reasons for them when we wish to justify them, but they are elemental, non-rational, precedent of thought. None the less may they be brought under control, and changed – though not directly.

Consider physical taste; an olive, preserved in brine, is offered to a child, and is generally rejected with disgust. But it is a fashionable thing to like olives, and your people persevere in eating them, determined to like them, and presently they are fond of them. They have changed their disliking to liking. How is the change of taste brought about? By the action of Will, directed by the mind.

xix. THE MASTERY OF DESIRE

We can change desires by thought. The desire nature with which we are born is good, bad, or indifferent, and it follows its own way in early childhood. Presently we examine it, and mark some desires as useful, others as useless or even noxious. We then form a mental image of the desire nature which would be useful and noble, and we deliberately set to work to create it by thought-power. There are some physical desires which we see will bring about disease if left uncontrolled: eating too much, because of the gratification of the palate; drinking alcoholic liquors, because they exhilarate and vivify; yielding to the pleasures of sex. We see in the persons of others that these cause obesity, shaken nerves, premature exhaustion. We determine not to yield to them; we bridle the horses of the senses with the bits and reins of the mind, and deliberately hold them in, although they struggle; if they are very refractory we call up the image of the glutton, the drunkard, the worn-out profligate, and so create a repulsion for the causes which made them what they are. And so with all other desires. Deliberately choose out and encourage those which lead to refining and elevating pleasures, and reject those which result in coarseness of body and of mind. There will be failures in your resistance, but in spite of failures, persevere. At first, you will yield to the desire, and only remember too late that you had resolved to abstain; persevere. Presently the desire and the memory of the good resolution will arise together, and there will be a period of struggle – your Kurukshetra – and you will sometimes succeed and sometimes fail; persevere. Then successes will multiply, and failures be few; persevere. Then desire dies, and you watch beside its tomb, lest it should only be entranced, and revive. Finally you have done with that form of desire for ever. You have worked with the law and have conquered.

xx. TWO OTHER POINTS

Students are sometimes troubled because in their dreams they yield to a vice which down here they have conquered, or feel the stirring of a desire which they thought long slain. Knowledge will destroy the trouble. In a dream, a man is in his astral body, and a stirring of desire, too weak to cause physical matter to vibrate, will cause a vibration in astral matter; let the dreamer resist, as he soon will if he determines to do so, and the desire will cease. Further, he should remember that there will be left for some time in the astral body effete matter, which was formerly used when the desire arose, but which is now, from disuse, in process of disintegration. This may be temporarily vivified by a passing desire-form and thus caused to vibrate artificially. This may happen to a man when he is either sleeping or waking. It is but the artificial movement of a corpse. Let him repudiate it: " Thou are not from me. Get thee gone." And the vibration will be stilled.

The warrior who is battling with desire must not let his mind dwell on the objects which arouse desire. Again, thought is creative. Thought will awaken desire, and stir it into vigorous activity. Of the man who abstained from action but enjoyed in thought, Shri Krishna sternly said: "That deluded man is called a hypocrite." Nourished by thought, desires cannot die. They will but become stronger by physical repression when fed by thought. It is better not to fight desire, but rather to evade it. If it arises, turn the mind to something else, to a book, a game, to anything which is at once pure and attractive. By fighting it, the mind dwells on it, and thus feeds and strengthens it. If you know that the desire is likely to arise, have ready something to which to turn at once. So shall it be starved out, having no nourishment of either act or thought.

Never let us forget that objects are desirable because of the immanence of God. "There is nothing moving or unmoving that can exist bereft of Me." At a certain stage of evolution, the attraction to them makes for progress. Only later on, are they superseded. The child plays with a doll; it is well; it draws out the germinal mother-love. But a grown woman playing with a doll would be pitiable. Objects of desire draw out emotions which aid in development, and stimulate exertion. They cease to be useful when we have grown beyond them, and in ceasing to be useful they become mischievous.

The bearing of all this on karma is self-evident. Since by desire we create opportunities and attract within our reach the objects of desire, our desires now map out our opportunities and our possessions hereafter. By harbouring none but pure desires, and wishing for naught that cannot be used in service, we ensure a future of opportunities for helping our fellows, and of possessions which shall be consecrated to the Master's work.

xxi. THE THIRD THREAD

We have now to consider how karma works in relation to activity, the third aspect of the Self. Our activities – the ways in which we affect the outer world of matter – spin the third thread of our karma, and in many respects this is the least important. Our thoughts and our desires so soon as they flow outwards, by producing vibrations in the mental and astral matter surrounding us, or by creating specific thought-forms and desire-forms, become activities, are our action on the outer worlds of life and form, of consciousness and bodies. The moment they speed outwards they affect other things and other people, they are the action, or the reaction as the case may be, of the organism on the environment. The reaction of our thoughts on ourselves, as we have seen, is the building of character and of faculty; the reaction of our desires on ourselves is the gaining of opportunities and objects and of power; the reaction of our activities on ourselves is our environment, the conditions and circumstances, the friends and enemies, that surround us. The nearest circumstance, the expression of part of our past activities, is our physical body; this is shaped for us by an elemental specially created for the task; our body is nature's answer to such part of the sum of our past activities as can be expressed in a single material form, and "nature" is here the Lords of Karma, the mighty Angels of Judgment, the Recorders of the Past. Two parts of karma we bring with us – our thought-nature and our desire-nature, the germinal tendencies we have created in our age-long past; the third part of karma we are born into; that which limits our Self-expression and constrains us; our past action on the external world reacts upon us as the sum of our limitations – our environment, including our physical body.

It is probable that a close study of past activities and present environment would result in a knowledge of details that at present we do not possess. We read in Buddhist and Hindu Scriptures a mass of details on this subject, probably drawn from meticulous careful observation. At present, we modern students can only affirm a few broad facts. Extreme cruelty inflicted on the helpless – on heretics, on children, on animals – reacts on inquisitors, on brutal parents and teachers, on vivisectors, as physical deformity, more or less revolting and extreme, according to the nature and extent of the cruelty.

xxii. PERFECT JUSTICE

From the physical agony inflicted results physical agony endured, for karma is the restoration of the equilibrium disturbed. Motive, in this region, does not mitigate, any more than the pain of a burn is mitigated because the injury has been sustained in saving a child from the fire. Where a good motive existed, however intellectually misdirected – as the saving of souls from the torture of hell, in the case of the inquisitor, or the saving of bodies from the torture of disease, in the case of the vivisector – it has its full result in the region of the character. Hence we may find a person born deformed, with a gentle and patient character, showing that in a past life he strove to see the right and did the wrong. The Angels of Judgment are utterly just, and the golden thread of completely misdirected love may gleam beside the black thread woven by cruelty; none the less will the black thread draw to the doer of cruelty a misshapen body. On the other hand, where lust of power and indifference to the pain of others have mingled their baleful influences with the infliction of cruelty, there will be found also a mental and emotional twist; a historical case is that of Marat, who, instead of expiating the cruelty of the past, intensified it by new cruelty in the very life in which he was reaping the harvest of previous evil. Hereditary and congenital diseases, again, are the reaction from past misdeeds. The drunkard of a previous life will be born into a family in which drunkenness has left diseases of the nerves – epilepsy and the like. The profligate will be born into a family tainted with diseases which spring from sexual vice. A "bad heredity" is the reaction from wrong activities in the past. Often the man who is reaping these sad harvests shows in his moral nature that he has purged himself from the evil, though the physical harvesting remains. A steadfast patience, a sweet enduring content, tell that the evil lies behind, that victory has been gained, though the wounds sustained in the conflict smart and sting. So may a soldier, sorely maimed in a fierce battle remain mutilated for the rest of his physical life, and yet not regret with any keenness the anguish and the loss which mark that he has gloriously discharged his duty to his Flag. And these warriors who have conquered in a greater battle need not lament too bitterly over the weakness or deformity of a body which tells of a strife which is past, but may wear patiently the badge of a struggle with an evil they have overcome, knowing that in another life no scar of that struggle shall remain.

XXIII. OUR ENVIRONMENT

The nation and the family into which a man is born give him the field suitable for the development of faculties he needs, or for the exercise of faculties he has gained, which are required for the helping of others at that place and time. Sometimes a strenuous life passed in the company of superiors, which has stimulated latent powers and quickened the growth of germinal faculties, is followed by one of ease amid ordinary people, in order to test the reality of the strength acquired and the solidity of the apparent conquest over self. Sometimes, when an ego has definitely gained certain mental faculties and has secured them as part of his mental equipment by sufficient practice, he will be born into surroundings where these are useless, and confronted by tasks of a most uncongenial nature. A man ignorant of karma will fret and fume, will perform grudgingly his distasteful duties, and will think regretfully of his "wasted talents, while that fool Jones is in a place which he is not fit to fill"; he does not realise that Jones has to learn a lesson which he himself has already mastered, and that he himself would not be evolving further by repeating over again that which he has already done. In a similar situation, the knower of karma will quietly study his surroundings, will realise that he would gain nothing by doing that which it would be easy for him to do – i.e., that which he has already done well in the past – and will address himself contentedly to the uncongenial work, seeking to understand what it has to teach him, and resolutely settling himself to learn the new lesson.

XXIV. OUR KITH AND KIN

So also with an ego who finds himself entangled with family responsibilities and duties, when he would fain spring forward to answer a call for helpers in a larger work. If ignorant of karma, he will fret against his bonds, or even break them, and thus ensure their return to the future. The knower of karma will see in these duties the reactions from his own past activities, and will patiently accept and discharge them; he knows that when they are fully paid, they will drop away from him and leave him free, and that meanwhile they have some lessons to teach him which it is incumbent upon him to learn; he will seek to see those lessons and to learn them, sure that the powers they evoke will make him a more efficient helper when he is free to answer to the call to which his whole nature is thrilling in response.

Again, the knower of karma will seek to establish in his nation and his family, conditions which will attract to each egos of an advanced and noble type. He will see to it that his household arrangements, its scrupulous cleanliness, its hygienic conditions, its harmony, good feeling, and loving-kindness, the purity of its mental and moral atmosphere, shall form a magnet of attraction, drawing towards it and into relationship with it egos of a high level, whether they be seeking embodiment – if young parents are members of the household – or be already in bodies, coming into the family as future husbands and wives, friends, or dependents. So far as his power extends, he will help in forming similar conditions in his town, his province, his country. He knows that egos must be born amid surroundings suitable for them, and that, therefore, by providing good surroundings he will attract egos of desirable type.

xxv. OUR NATION

With regard to national environment, the knower of karma must carefully study the national conditions into which he is born, in order to see whether he is born therein chiefly to develop qualities in which he is deficient, or chiefly to help his nation by qualities well developed in himself. In times of transition, many egos may be born into a nation, with qualities of the type of required in the new conditions into which that nation is passing. Thus, in America, which will presently develop the beginnings of a Commonwealth in which cooperation shall replace competition, there have been born a number of egos of vast organising ability, of highly developed will power, and keen commercial intelligence; they have created Trusts, organisations of industry built with consummate ability, manifesting the economical advantages of doing away with competition, of controlling production and supply, of meeting, but not over-meeting, demand. They have thus opened the way to cooperative production and distribution, and prepared for a happier future. Soon will be born the egos who will see in the securing of the comfort of the nation a greater stimulus than personal gain, and they will complete the transition process; the one set have gathered into a head the forces of individualism; the other set will bend these forces to the common good.

Thus is environment governed by karma, and by a knowledge of law the desired environment may be created. If it grips us when once called into being, it is none the less ours to decide what that being shall be. Our power over that future environment is now in our hands, for its creator is the activities of the present.

xxvi. THE LIGHT FOR A GOOD MAN

Here is the light for a good man who finds himself surrounded by unhappy conditions. He has made his character, and he has also made his circumstances. His good thoughts and desires have made him what he is; the misdirection of them has created the environment through which he suffers. Let him, then, not be satisfied with being good, but see to it also that his influence on all around him is beneficial. Then shall it react on him as good environment. For instance: a mother is very unselfish, and she spoils her son by yielding, at her own cost, to all his whims, aiding him not at all to overcome his own selfish inclinations, fostering the lower nature, starving the higher. The son grows up selfish, uncontrolled, the slave of his own whims and desires. He causes unhappiness in the home, perchance brings upon it debt and disgrace. This reaction is the environment she created by her unwisdom, and she must bear the distresses it brings upon her.

A selfish man may, on the other hand, create for himself in the future an environment regarded as fortunate by the world. With the hope of gaining a title, he builds a hospital and equips it fully; many sufferers therein find relief, many sick unto death have their last moments soothed, many children are lovingly nursed back into health. The reaction from all this will be easy and pleasant surroundings for himself; he will reap the harvest of the physical good which he has sown. But his selfishness will also sow according to its kind, and mentally and morally he will reap that harvest also, a harvest of disappointment and of pain.

xxvii. KNOWLEDGE OF LAW

The knowledge of karma will not only enable a man to build, as he wills, his own future, but it will also enable him to understand the workings of karmic law in the cases of others, and thus more effectively to help them. Only by knowledge of law can we move fearlessly and usefully in worlds where law is inviolable, and, secure ourselves, enable others to reach a similar security. In the physical world the supremacy of law is universally admitted, and the man who disregards "natural law" is regarded not as a criminal but as a fool. Equal is the folly, and more far-reaching, of disregarding "natural law" in the worlds above the physical, and of imagining that, while law in the physical world is omnipresent, the mental and moral worlds are lawless and disorderly. In those worlds, as in the physical, law is inviolable and omnipresent, and of all is it true:

Though the mills of God grind slowly, yet they grind exceeding Small;

Though with patience He stands waiting, with exactness Grinds He all.

We have seen that our present is the outcome of our past, that by thought we have built our character, by desires our opportunities of satisfying them, by actions our environment. Let us now consider how far we can modify in the present these results of our past, how far we are compelled, how far we are free.

xxviii. THE OPPOSING SCHOOLS

In the thought of the outer world, quite apart from the ideas of reincarnation and karma, there has been much opposing opinion. Robert Owen and his school regarded man as the creation of circumstances, ignoring heredity, that faint scientific reflection of karma; they considered that by changing the environment the man could be changed, most effectively if the child were taken ere he had formed bad habits; a child taken out of evil surroundings and placed amid good ones would grow into a good man. The failure of Robert

Owen's social experiment showed that his theory did not contain all the truth. Others, realising the force of heredity, almost ignored environment; "Nature," said Ludwig Buchner, "is stronger than nurture." In both these extreme views there is truth. Inasmuch as the child brings with him the nature built in his past, but dons the garment of a new mentality and a new emotional nature, in which his self-created faculties and qualities exist indeed, but as germs, not as fully developed powers, these germs may be nourished into rapid growth or atrophied by lack of nourishment, and this is wrought by the influence of the environment for good or ill. Moreover, the child puts on also the garment of a new physical body, with its own physical heredity, designed for the expression of some of the powers he brings with him, and this can be largely affected by his environment, and developed healthily or unhealthily. These facts were on the side of Robert Owen's theory, and they explain the successes gained by such philanthropic institutions as Dr. Barnardo's Homes, wherein germs of good are cultured and germs of evil are starved out. But the congenital criminal, and beings of that ilk, none may redeem in a single life, and these, of various grades, are the nonsuccesses of the benevolent rescuer.

Equally true is it, as the opposite school affirmed, that inborn character is a force with which every educationalist must reckon; he cannot create faculties which are not there; he cannot wholly eradicate evil tendencies which, below the surface, throw out roots, seeking appropriate nourishment; some nourishment reaches them from the thought-atmosphere around, from the evil desire-forms which arise from the evil in) others, forms of thoughts and desires which float in the air around, and cannot wholly be shut out – save by occult means, unknown to the ordinary educationalist.

xxix. THE MORE MODERN VIEW

The more modern scientific view that organism and environment act and react upon each other, each modifying the other, and that from the modifications new actions and reactions arise, and so on perpetually, takes in that which is true in each of the earlier views; it only needs to be expanded by the recognition of an enduring consciousness passing from life to life bringing its past with it, ever-growing, ever-evolving, and with its growth and evolution becoming an ever more and more potent factor in the direction and control of its future destiny.

Thus we reach the Theosophic standpoint; we cannot now help that which we have brought with us, nor can we help the environment into which we have been thrown; but we can modify both, and the more we know, the more effectively can we modify.

xxx. **SELF-EXAMINATION**

The first step is deliberately to examine what we may call our "stock in trade"; our inborn faculties and qualities, good and bad, our powers and our weaknesses, our present opportunities, our actual environment. Our character is that which is most rapidly modifiable, and on this we should set to work, selecting the qualities which it is desirable to strengthen, the weaknesses which form our most pressing dangers. We take them one by one, and use our thought-power in the way before described, remembering always that we must never think of the weakness, but of its corresponding power. We think that which we desire to be, and gradually, inevitably, we become it. The law cannot fail; we have only to work with it in order to succeed.

The desire-nature is similarly modified by thought, and we create the thought-forms of the opportunities we need; alert to see and to grasp a suitable opportunity, our will also fixes itself on the forms our thought creates, and thus draws them within reach, literally making and then grasping the opportunities which the karma of the past does not present to us.

Hardest of all to change is our environment, for here we are dealing with the densest form of matter, that on which our thought-force is least potent. Here our freedom is very restricted, for we are at our weakest and the past is at its strongest. Yet are we not wholly helpless, for here, either by struggling or by yielding, we can conquer in the end. Such undesirable part of our surroundings as we can change by strenuous effort, we promptly set to work to change; that which we cannot thus change, we accept, and set ourselves to learn whatever it has to teach. When we have learnt its lesson, it will drop away from us, like an outworn garment. We have an undesirable family; well, these are the egos we have drawn around us by our past; we fulfill every obligation cheerfully and patiently, honourably paying our debts; we acquire patience through the annoyances they inflict on us, fortitude through their daily irritations, forgiveness through their wrongs. We use them as a sculptor uses his tools, to chip off our excrescences and to smooth and polish away our roughnesses. When their usefulness to us is over, they will be removed by circumstances, carried off elsewhere. And so with other parts of our environment, which, on the surface, are distressful; like a skillful sailor, who trims his sails to a wind he cannot change and thus forces it to carry him on his way, we use the circumstances we cannot alter by adapting ourselves to them in such a fashion that they are compelled to help us.

Thus we are partly compelled and partly free. We must work amid and with the conditions which we have created, but we are free within them to work upon them. We ourselves, eternal Spirits, are inherently free, but we can only work in and through the thought-nature, the desire-nature, and the physical nature, which we have created; these are our materials and our tools, and we can have none other till we make these anew.

XXXI. OUT OF THE PAST

Another point of great importance to remember is that the karma of the past is of very mixed character; we have not to breast a single current, the totality of the past, but a stream made up of currents running in various directions, some opposing us, some helping us; the effective force we have to face, the resultant left when all these opposition have neutralized each other, may be one which it is by no means beyond our present power to overcome. Face to face with a piece of evil karma from the past, we should ever grapple with it, striving to overcome it, remembering that it embodies only a part of our past, and that other parts of that same past are with us, strengthening and invigorating us for the contest. The present effort, added to those forces from the past, may be, often is, just enough to overcome the opposition.

Or, again, an opportunity presents itself, and we hesitate to take advantage of it, fearing that our resources are inadequate to discharge the responsibilities it brings; but it would not be there unless our karma had brought it to us, the fruit of a past desire; let us seize it, bravely and tenaciously, and we shall find that the very effort has awakened latent powers slumbering within us, unknown to us, and needing a stimulus from outside to arouse them into activity. So many of our powers, created by effort in the past, are on the verge of expression, and only need opportunity to flower into action.

We should always aim at a little more than we think we can do – not at a thing wholly beyond our present powers, but at that which seems to be just out of reach. As we work to achieve it, all the karmic force acquired in the past comes to our aid to strengthen us. The fact that we can nearly do a thing means that we have worked for it in the past, and the accumulated strength of those past efforts is within us. That we can do a little means the power of doing more; and even if we fail, the power put forth to the utmost passes into the reservoir of our forces, and the failure of today means the victory of tomorrow

When circumstances are adverse, the same thing holds good; we may have reached the point where one more effort means success. Therefore did Bhishma counsel effort under all conditions, and utter the encouraging phrase; "Exertion is greater than destiny." The result of many past exertions is embodied in our karma, and the present exertion added to them may make our force adequate for the achievement of our aim.

There are cases where the force of the karma of the past is so strong that no effort of the present can suffice to overbear it. Yet should effort be made, since few know when one of these cases is upon them, and, at the worst, the effort made diminishes that karmic force for the future. A chemist often labours for years to discover a force, or an arrangement of matter, which will enable him to achieve a result at which he is aiming. He is often thwarted, but he does not acknowledge himself defeated. He cannot change the chemical elements; he cannot change the laws of chemical combination; he accepts these ungrudgingly, and there lies "the sublime patience of the investigator". But the knowledge of the investigator, ever increasing by virtue of his patient experiments, at last touches the point where it enables him to bring about the desired result. Precisely the same spirit should be acquired by the student of karma; he should accept the inevitable without complaint, but untiredly seek the methods whereby his aim may be secured, sure that his only limitation is his ignorance, and that perfect knowledge must mean perfect power.

XXXII. OLD FRIENDSHIPS

Another fact of the greatest importance is that we are brought by karma in touch with people whom we have known in the past, to some of whom we owe debts, some of whom owe debts to us. No man treads his long pilgrimage alone, and the egos to whom he is linked by many ties in a common past come from all parts of the world to surround him in the present. We have known some one in the past who has gone ahead of us in evolution; perchance we then did him some service, and a karmic tie was formed. In the present, that tie draws us within the orbit of his activity, and we receive from outside us a new impulse of force, a power, not our own, impelling us to listen and to obey.

Many of such helpful karmic links have we seen within the Theosophical Society. Long, long ago, He who is the Master K.H. was taken prisoner in a battle with an Egyptian army, and was generously befriended and sheltered by an Egyptian of high rank. Thousands of years later, help is needed for the nascent Theosophical Society, and the Master, looking over India for one to aid in this great work, sees His old friend of the Egyptian and other lives, now Mr. A.P. Sinnett, editing the leading Anglo-Indian newspaper, The Pioneer. Mr. Sinnett goes, as usual, to Simla; Mme Blavatsky goes up thither, to form the link; Mr. Sinnett is drawn within the immediate influence of the Master, receives instruction from Him, and becomes the author of *The Occult World* and of *Esoteric Buddhism*, carrying to thousands the message of Theosophy. Such rights we win by help given in the past, the right to help in higher ways and with further reaching effects, while we ourselves are also helped by the tightening of ancient links of friendship won by service, royally recompensed by that priceless gift of knowledge, gained by one and shed abroad for many.

XXXIII. WE GROW BY GIVING

In truth, in this world of law, where action and reaction are equal, all help which is given comes back to the giver, as a ball thrown against a wall bounds back to the hand of the thrower. That which we give returns to us; hence, even for a selfish reason, it is well to give, and to give abundantly. "Cast thy bread upon the waters, and thou shalt find it after many days," To give, even from a selfish motive, is good, for it leads to an interchange of worthy human feelings, by which both giver and receiver grow and expand, so that the Divine within each has opportunity of larger expression. Even though the gift, at first, be a matter of calculation – "He that hath pity upon the poor lendeth unto the Lord: and look, what he layeth out, it shall be paid him again" – yet gradually the love evoked shall make future giving spontaneous and unselfish, and thus karmic links of love shall bind ego to ego in the long series of human lives. All personal links, whether of love or hate, grow out of the past, and in each life we strengthen the ties that bind us to our friends and ensure our return together in the lives that lie in front. Thus do we build up a true family, outside all ties of blood, and return to earth over and over again to knit closer the ancient bonds.

xxxiv. COLLECTIVE KARMA

Before completing this imperfect study we must consider what is termed Collective Karma, the complex into which are woven the results of the collective thoughts, desires and activities of groups, whether large or small. The principles at work are the same, but the factors are far more numerous, and this multiplicity immensely increases the difficulty of understanding the effects.

The idea of considering a group as a larger individual is not alien from modern science, and such larger individuals generate karma along lines similar to those which we have been studying. A family, a nation, a sub-race, a race, are all but larger individuals, each having a past behind it, the creator of its present, each with a future ahead of it, now in course of creation. An ego coming into such a larger individual must share in its general karma; his own special karma has brought him into it, and must be worked out within it, the larger karma often offering conditions which enable the smaller to act.

xxxv. FAMILY KARMA

Let us consider the collective karma of a family. The family has a thought-atmosphere of its own, into the colouring of which enter family traditions and customs, family ways of regarding the external world, family pride in the past, a strong sense of family honour. All the thought-forms of a member of the family will be influenced by these conditions, built up perhaps through hundreds of years, and shaping, moulding, colouring, all the thoughts, desires and activities of the individual newly born into it. Tendencies in him that conflict with family traditions will be suppressed, all unconsciously to him; the things "a fellow cannot do" will have for him no attraction; he will be lifted above various temptations, and the seeds of evil which such temptations might have vivified in him will quietly atrophy away. The collective karma of the family will provide him with opportunities for distinction, open out avenues of usefulness, bring him advantages in the struggle for life, and ensure his success. How has he come into conditions so favourable? It may be by a personal tie with some one already there, a service rendered in a previous life, a bond of affection, an unexhausted relationship. This avails to draw him into the circle, and he then profits by the various karmic results which belong to the family in virtue of its collective past, of the courage, ability, usefulness of some of its members, that have left an inheritance of social consideration as a family heirloom.

Where the family karma is bad the individual born into it suffers, as in the former case he profits, and the collective karma hinders, as in the former instance it promoted, his welfare.

In both cases the individual will usually have built up in himself characteristics which demand for their full exercise the environment provided by the family. But a very strong personal tie, or unusual service, might, without this, draw a man into a family wherein was his beneficiary, and so give him an opportunity which, generally, he has not deserved, but had won by this special act of his past.

xxxvi. NATIONAL KARMA

Let us think on the collective karma of a nation. Face to face with this, the individual is comparatively helpless, for nothing he can do can free him from this, and he must trim his sails to it as best he may. Even a Master can but slightly modify national karma, or change the national atmosphere.

The rise and fall of nations are brought about by collective karma. Acts of national righteousness or of national criminality, led up to by noble or base thinking, largely directed by national ideals, bring about national ascent or national descent. The actions of the Spanish

Inquisition, the driving of the Jews and of the Moors out of Spain, the atrocious cruelties accompanying the conquests of Mexico and Peru – all these were national crimes, which dragged Spain down from its splendid position of power, and reduced it to comparative powerlessness.

Seismic changes – earthquakes, volcanoes, floods – or national catastrophes like famine and plague, all are cases of collective karma, brought about by great streams of thoughts and actions of a collective rather than an individual character.

As with a family, so with a nation to a much greater degree, will there be an atmosphere created by the nation's past; and national traditions, customs, viewpoints, will exercise a vast influence on the minds of all who dwell within the nation. Few individuals can free themselves wholly from these influences, and consider a question affecting the nation without any bias, or see it from a standpoint other than that of their own people. Hence largely arise international quarrels and suspicions, mistaken views, and distorted opinions of the motives of another nation. Many a war has broken out in consequence of the differences in the thought-atmospheres surrounding the prospective combatants, and these difficulties are multiplied when the nations spring from different racial stocks, as, say, the Italians and the Turks. All the knower of karma can do, in these cases, is to realise the fact that his opinions and views are largely the product of the larger individuality of his nation, and to check this bias as much as he can, giving full weight to the views obtained from the standpoint of the antagonistic nation.

When a man finds himself in the grip of a national karma which he cannot resist – say that he is a member of a conquered nation – he should calmly study the causes which have led to the national subjugation, and should set to work to remedy them, endeavouring to influence public opinion along lines which will eradicate these causes.

XXXVII. INDIA'S KARMA

There was an article published in *East and West* – Mr. Malabari's paper – some time ago on the national karma of India, which was an admirable example of the way in which national karma should not be regarded. It was said that the national karma of India was that it should be conquered – obviously true, else the conquest of India would not have taken place – and that it should therefore accept its lot of service, and not try to change any of the existing conditions – as obviously wrong. The knower of karma would say: The Indians were not the original possessors of this country; they came down from Central Asia, conquering the land, subduing its then peoples, and reducing them to servitude; during thousands of years they conquered and ruled, and they generated a national karma. They trod down the conquered tribes, and made them slaves, oppressing them and taking advantage of them. The bad karma thus made brought down upon them in turn many invaders. Greeks, Mughals, Portuguese, Dutch, French, English – they all came, and fought, and conquered, and possessed. Still the lesson of karma has not been learned, though the millions of the untouchables are a standing proof of the wrongs inflicted upon them. Now the Indians ask for a share in the government of their own country, and they are hampered by this bad national karma. Let them, then, while asking for the growth of freedom for themselves, atone to these untouchables by giving them social freedom and lifting them in the social scale. A national effort must remove this national evil, and do away with a continuing cause of national weakness. India must redeem the wrong she has done, and cleanse her hands from oppression; so shall she change her national karma, and build the foundation of freedom. Karma will work for freedom and not against it, when the karma generated by oppression is changed into the karma made by uplifting and respecting. Public feeling can be changed, and every man who speaks graciously and kindly to an inferior is helping to change it. Meanwhile all whose own individual karma has brought them into the nation should recognise facts as they are, but should set to work to change those that are undesirable. National karma may be changed, like individual karma, but as the causes are of longer continuance, so must be the effects, and the new causes introduced can only slowly modify the results outgrowing from the past.

XXXVIII. NATIONAL DISASTERS

The karma which brings about seismic catastrophes and other national disasters includes in its sweep vast numbers of individuals whose special karma contains sudden death, disease, or prolonged physical suffering. It is interesting and instructive to notice the way in which people who have not such karmic liabilities are called away from the scene of a great catastrophe, while others are hurried into it; when an earthquake slays a number of people there will be cases of "miraculous escape" – one called away by a telegram, by urgent business, etc. – and of equally miraculous tossing of victims into the place in time for their slaying. If such calling away proved to be impossible, then some special arrangement at the moment guarded from death, a beam, keeping off falling stones, or the like.

When a natural catastrophe is impending, people with appropriate individual karma are gathered together in the place, as in the flood at Johnstown, Pa., or the great earthquake and fire at San Francisco. In an earthquake in the north of India a few years ago, there were some victims who had posted back in hot haste – to be killed. Others left the place the night before – to be saved from death. The local catastrophe is used to work off particular karmas. Or a carriage taking a man to the station is stopped in a street block, and he misses the train. He is angry, but the train is wrecked and he is saved. It is not that the block was there in order to stop him, but that the block was utilised for the purpose. At Messina some who were not to die were dug out days afterwards, and in more than one case food had come to maintain life, brought by an astral agent. In shipwrecks, again, safety or death will depend on individual karma. Sometimes an ego has a debt of sudden death to pay, but it has not been included in the debts to be discharged during the present incarnation; but his presence in some accident brought about by a collective karma offers the opportunity of discharging the debt "out of due time". The ego prefers to seize the opportunity and to get rid of the karma, and his body is struck away with the rest.

xxxix. HOW THE EGO SELECTS

Individual characteristics developed in one life may bring their owner in another life into a nation which offers peculiar facilities for their exercise. Thus a man who had developed a strong concrete mind, apt for commerce, say, in the vaishya (merchant) caste in India, may be thrown down into the United States of America, and there become a Rockefeller. In his new personality he will see that vast wealth is only tolerable when used for national purposes, and he will carry out in

America the vaishya ideal that the man who has gathered huge wealth becomes a steward in the national household, to distribute wisely for the general benefit the stores accumulated as personal possessions. Thus the old ideal will be planted in the midst of a new civilisation, and will spread abroad through another people.

XL. ENGLAND'S KARMA

A colonizing nation, like England, will often be guilty of much cruelty in the seizing of lands belonging to the savage tribes that the colonists drive out. Thousands perish prematurely during the conquest and subsequent settlement. These have a karmic claim against England collectively, as well as the debts due from the actual assailants. They are drawn to England and take birth in her slums, providing a population of congenital criminals, of non-moral and feeble-minded people.

The debt due to them by the summary closing of their previous existences should be paid by education and training, thus quickening their evolution and lifting them out of their natural savagery.

XLI. THE FRENCH REVOLUTION

The collective selfishness and indifference of the well-to-do towards the poor and miserable, leaving them to fester in overcrowded slums, among degrading and evil-provoking surroundings, bring down upon themselves social troubles, labour unrest, threatening combinations. Carried to excess in France during the reigns of Louis XIV and Louis XV, this same selfishness and indifference were the direct causes of the French Revolution, of the destruction of the Crown and of the nobility.

Taught by Theosophy to see the workings of karmic law in the history of nations as well as in that of individuals, we should be forces making for national welfare and prosperity. The strongest karmic cause is the power of thought, and this is as true for nations as for individuals.

XLII. A NOBLE NATIONAL IDEAL

To hold up a noble national ideal is to set going the most powerful karmic force, for into such an ideal the thoughts of many are ever flowing, and it becomes stronger by the daily influx. Public opinion continually changes under the flow of its influences, and reproduces that which is constantly held up for its admiration. The thought-force accumulates until it becomes irresistible and lifts the whole nation upwards to a higher level.

The knowers of karma can work deliberately and consciously, sure of their ground, sure of their methods, relying on the Good Law. Thus they become conscious cooperators with the Divine Will which works in evolution, and are filled with a deep peace and an unending joy.

BOOK FOUR
ELEMENTARY LESSONS
ON KARMA

FEW questions, perhaps, puzzle students more, whether the students be old or young, than that of Karma. What is it? when did it begin? how far does it limit us? are we its servants or its masters? must we fold our hands meekly before it, or struggle vigorously against it? if today grows out of yesterday, and yesterday out of the day before, and so on, backwards and backwards, how can the bad man ever become good? are we not really compelled by an iron necessity, are we not " dumb, driven cattle," who cannot become heroes, whatever poets may say?

We may spend a little time usefully in thinking over these questions and others resembling them, for here, as elsewhere, " a little knowledge is a dangerous thing ". Karma is but too often a crippling fetter instead of being, as it ought to be, a strength, a guide, a force, enabling us to act wisely and well. Like all other laws in nature, it binds the ignorant and gives power to the wise.

Here is our first step: Karma is a Law of Nature. We might go further, and say: It is *the* law. For it is everywhere and always — omnipresent, all-pervasive. Other names are given to it in the West, and the names are useful, because they are not surrounded by all the traditions and discussions which blur the meaning of karma in the East. The Western philosopher calls it *The Law of Causation*. He sees in every happening a double fact — it is both an effect and a cause; it is an effect, for it has a cause; something went before and made this thing to happen; it is also a cause; for it will generate a new happening, another thing will arise from it. As a man is a son of his father, and is also the father of his son; as his father was a son to his own father, and as his son will be a father to his own son in turn, so is it with causes and effects; each event is at once an effect and a cause — an effect of the past, a cause of the future. This observed succession, this invariable relation, is generalized under the term, the law of causation. The human intellect recognizes this law as fundamental, and sees in it the assurance of stability and order as well as of human progress.

We are continually causing effects, unconsciously and consciously. The more we understand our power and nature's conditions, the more can we bring about the effects we desire, and prevent the events we dislike.

The Western scientist calls karma, *The Law of Action and Re-action*, and he also sees it as a fundamental law. *Action and Re-action are equal and opposite*, he says. You push an object; its resistance is its re-action against your push; you fling an elastic ball against a board; it springs back to you with a force proportional to that of the impact. Everywhere in nature he finds this law, and he counts on it with certainty in his manipulations of objects.

In both these Western terms the word *Law* appears. What is a Law — a Law of Nature? It is the statement of an observed succession, of an invariable sequence; it may be put as a formula; wherever A and B are, there C follows. Hence it is a statement of conditions, and the result which arises from them. It is not a *command*; it does not say "Do this, *or* Do not do this," like a human enactment. It does not say: " You must have A and B, and therefore C; " but rather: " If you want C, you must bring A and B together; if you do not want C, you must take care that A and B do not come together; if you keep A away from B, you will not have C." Hence a law of nature is truly said to be not a compelling but an enabling force; it tells you the conditions which enable you to produce or avoid a particular thing, and is only compulsory in this sense, that *if* you make the conditions you *must* have the result. Because of this inevitable sequence ignorant people are helpless in the grip of natural laws; they ignorantly produce conditions, and the results hurtle around them, confuse and crush them. As we gain knowledge, we take care as to the conditions we produce, and thus avoid undesirable results.

A law of Nature is said to be inviolable, for this relation between cause and effect cannot be altered. We can disregard natural laws as much as we please, but the law breaks us; we do not break it. If you slip off the top of a building and fall heavily to the ground, you do not break the law of attraction, or gravitation; you disregard it, and your fall proves its truth; a well known formula gives the velocity with which you will strike the ground.

We partly answer, then, our first question, "what is karma?" by the statement: karma is a law of nature of universal validity, called in the West the law of causation, or the law of action and re-action.

The remainder of the answer to the question, "what is karma?" is very closely connected with the second question: "When did karma begin?" A general law of nature cannot be said to have either a beginning, or an ending; wherever there is any manifestation, any universe, any world, there, general laws are also present, inherent in the very nature of things. Attraction of one mass of matter to another cannot be said to *begin*; wherever there are masses of matter, there, attraction is working; gravitation does not *begin*, it is ever manifested where the conditions for its working are present. Hence karma, being, a general Law, is said to be eternal; it is a condition of manifested existence, and wherever existence is manifested, there is karma.

Hence the question: "When did karma begin?" shows a misconception of the very nature of karma; it is a perpetual condition of existence in matter, neither beginning nor ending, but eternal. If the form of the question be modified, and it is asked: "When did the karma of a particular creature begin?" then the answer is: "At the time at which that particular creature came into manifestation." When the unborn, undying Spirit takes to himself a vesture of matter, then he steps into conditions, and comes under the law of karma. His stepping into the conditions begins his particular karma. At first it will be the karma of a mineral, the play upon him of surrounding force and matter, and the re-action from him on his surroundings. These actions and re-actions weave the links of his karma, and the chain draws him into one or another type of the vegetable kingdom. In that, as his re-action becomes more complex, the web of karma attaching to him becomes more complicated, and ultimately lifts him into some animal type. In the animal kingdom his increasing sentiency enters into karmic causes, and pains inflicted by him re-act as pains on him. But the feeling of pain is due to the evolution of the power to feel in him; it is still action and re-action, but where in the mineral these were unaccompanied by feeling, in the animal, feeling results in pleasure and pain: the law is the same; the creature is different, and so the result on the creature is different. As reason develops, another stand is added to the karmic web, and the action in the thought world is added to that in the acting and feeling worlds, and hence another powerful factor is added to the reaction. But once again, the law of action and reaction is working on the same lines.

If the student will constantly bear in mind that karma is action and re-action, and that this works on every plane of nature, works everywhere and always, and is inherent in the nature of things, many of his difficulties will disappear; he will understand that karma begins for him when he descends into the universe of matter, because he has come into the conditions in which karma is perpetually working, and that the re-actions on him are exactly equal to his actions, containing more or fewer factors according to those which have gone out from himself.

Another thing that will become clear to him is that the re-action must be of the same nature as the action; hence when a man commits a mistaken act with a good motive, his action is on three planes, the physical, the astral and the mental; the re-action must also be on three planes; the mental re-action will be on his character, which will be improved by the impact of good upon it; the astral re-action will make for him future opportunity of exercising right desire; both these will be good; but the re-action upon the physical plane of the mistaken act will be misfortune to himself. Thus the law works with perfect accuracy and inviolability, and the re-action upon each action follows in unvarying succession.

The idea of rewards and punishments ought not to be allowed to enter into the workings of karmic law. We have results, consequences, but neither rewards nor punishments. Pain is the outcome of wrong activity on any plane, not because anyone inflicts pain upon us as a punishment, but because we have flung ourselves against the law and are bruised against its unyieldingness. The result of virtuous thought or feeling is an increase of the capacity to be virtuous; it is not prosperity, either in this world or another. If we tell a lie, the result is the increased tendency to falsehood, the lowering of our character, and this is an invariable result, not affected by the discovery or otherwise of our falsity by those around us; their want of trust is the re-action from their discovery of our lie; the re-action on us of the increased tendency to falsehood is independent of this secondary result.

"How far does the law of karma limit us?" — such is the question now to be considered, and it falls naturally into two parts: (1) The limiting action of laws of nature, of which karma is one; (2) The limiting action of the special karma which each one of us has generated in the past. We have already seen that a law of nature is a sequence of conditions, and the conditions among which we find ourselves impose upon us certain limitations. Thus a man cannot fly under ordinary conditions, and if he desires to travel through the air he must supply himself with some apparatus by which he can rise into the air and move therein. The more we know of the natural forces around us, the greater is our freedom of movement amongst them, for we can balance one against the other, neutralizing those which are opposed to any course which we wish to take. If we wish to descend from a tower to the ground by jumping from the top, the conditions are such as to result in the fracture of our bones if we merely jump into the air; but if we arm ourselves with a parachute of sufficient size, we may safely launch ourselves into the air, and float gradually down to the earth. Again, we cannot rise above the atmosphere, and long before reaching its upper regions we should find the air too rare to be respirable; here is a limiting condition; but, on the other hand, we could overcome this limitation by taking with us a supply of respirable air. The power of natural conditions to limit us can very largely be overcome by knowledge, and the larger our knowledge the more freely can we act. Exactly the same is true with regard to the universal conditions called karma; we are limited by them as by the other conditions found in nature, but can neutralize or transcend these to a great extent by knowledge. Hence the enormous importance of studying and understanding the general karmic conditions, since our freedom is proportionate to our knowledge. Of more pressing and immediate importance is the limiting action of the special karma which each one of us has generated in the past, and an understanding of this is vital for the welfare of our life and the control of our conduct. This understanding will best be gained by a study of the working of karma along the three lines of character, opportunity and circumstances, generated by the three aspects of consciousness — thought, desire, and activity. In the whole of this study it must be remembered that we, who created this karma by our thought, desire and activity in the past, are the same thinking, desiring and acting consciousness in the present; people think too much of karma as reaction on them, and not sufficiently of their own action upon karmic conditions; we modify the outcome of past thinkings by present thinking, of past desires by present desire, of past actings by present acting. Kârmic action is not on an inert wall, but on a living consciousness, which reacts on karma and modifies it by that reaction. The passive endurance of karma is seen, and not the active impact upon it; thus a one-sided and inadequate view is taken, and man is paralyzed when he ought to be energizing.

An examination of each of the lines above-mentioned will enable us clearly to see how far karma limits us.

Thought makes character, such is the familiar and true statement. "As a man thinks, so he becomes." The character built up by thought in past lives is born with us in the present life. That we cannot escape, and it is a clear limitation. Let us say that we are born with poor mental abilities; these limit our capacity for acquiring knowledge, and we find ourselves compelled to spend two or three hours in mastering a lesson that our clever neighbour learns in ten minutes. There is a fact, a limitation, which undoubtedly exists. How can we deal with it? For the present we acquiesce in the fact; it is our karma. But, if we know the law, we shall at once begin to exercise our faculties, such as they are, to the full: we shall exert ourselves to the utmost, making up in time what we lack in power. Gradually the limits begin to widen out; thought is exerting its creative power, and our faculties improve under our strenuous cultivation. Accepting the limitation imposed by our poor thinking in the past, we sedulously work at its extension by better thinking now, and thus build up gradually an improved mental equipment for use in the future. Or we may have been born with an irritable temper; contrasting ourselves with a sweet-tempered neighbour, we are keenly conscious of our inferiority; again we feel our karmic limitation. But again we decline to sit down passively within it; we determinedly think patience, until at last we have created it as a faculty, and it becomes our habitual self-expression. Karma may hand on to us our wages for the past in the form of limitations, but karma cannot keep us within that area if we resolutely determine to break them down; within those limits we must begin, but we can change them by the very force which created them.

Desire, makes opportunity: such is the second familiar law. We may have been born clever, but opportunity to show our ability may be lacking; or we may make efforts which fail of success through *bad luck* rather than through defective workmanship. Clearly we are here hemmed in by a limitation; karma is frustrating our endeavours. Here, again, we must meet the limitation by resistant and persevering effort; we must back up our effort by strong desire, and *will* the success which eludes our grasp. Gradually we shall create opportunities and conquer our fate, and the limitations will widen out and the obstacles disappear.

Action makes circumstances is the third law. Most difficult of all are the limitations imposed by circumstances; but these also may slowly be changed. The best way is to accept them cheerfully and bravely, adapting ourselves within the limitations from which at first we cannot escape, but keeping up against them a quiet steady pressure, which slowly modifies them. Above all, we should try to increase the happiness of those around us, thinking little of our own, for past selfishness has made present misfortune, and the changing of the cause will bring about a changed effect. Within the present evil live sow the seed of future good, and within the limitations made by the past we create freedom for the future.

We will next consider the bearing on this question of Bhîshrna's famous phrase: *Exertion is greater than Destiny*.

Past exertions have made present destiny, present destiny may be changed by fresh exertions. A study of the conditions of such changing will complete our answer to the question: " How far does the law of karma limit us?"

We have seen that *thought makes character* . We look at our own character, and we see that we are deficient in truth, courage and gentleness. How shall we supply this deficiency since it is our karma to be untruthful, timid, and irritable. Thought is our tool for building up what we lack. Every morning we sit down quietly for five minutes and we think about truth. We say to ourselves: "Truth is Brahman; everything rests on truth. In my real Self I am truth, for I am divine. My mind, my body, must express my real Self. Today, I will think truthfully and accurately. I will say nothing untrue. I will do nothing that makes a false impression. o Thou who art Truth, and art my Self, shine out in me as Truth, and help me to be true." Then, during the day, we try to be on our guard against thinking, speaking, or acting untruthfully.

If we exaggerate anything, our morning thought will come up in the mind, and we shall at once feel that we have been untruthful. In such a case, we should deliberately and openly correct the false statement, though we shall feel a little bit ashamed of ourselves in doing so, and this will make us more careful next time. Thus we should go on, day after day, week after week, until we have established a habit of truthfulness in thought, word and deed, and we find, to our delight, that we are instinctively truthful, and the deficiency has vanished, the virtue of truth is ours.

Then we begin, all over again, to build up courage. We think about it in the morning, we practise it during the day. When we feel timid we say to ourselves: "Brahman is fearless, my Self is fearless; my mind and body must be brave." We read about brave people, and dwell on the value of courage. If we see a child or an animal ill-used, we do not slink out of the way, and say: "It is not my business." We go boldly up, and speak gently but firmly to the cruel person, and try to protect the helpless creature he is ill-using. After a time we find that timidity has disappeared, and we have become courageous.

Then we begin again once more to substitute gentleness for irritability; we think on gentleness every morning, we practice it during the day. If a person speaks to us sharply, and our irritable temper starts up all aflame, we force ourselves to be silent, not to answer back; when we can do this without effort, then we begin to answer gently, to soothe the ruffled feelings of the other, until at last we can bear any annoyance without impatience or irritation.

Another very good way of thinking in the morning, is to imagine ourselves perfectly truthful, or perfectly brave, or perfectly gentle. The imagination creates, and we become the model of the virtue which we have imagined ourselves to be. We think of ourselves as the *very perfect knight*, truthful, brave and gentle, and we become that which we think. By this use of the law of thought we have created new karma, and it has become our karma to be truthful, courageous, gentle. We have established this as our settled character, and we shall be born with it when we return to earth next time. Karma may compel us to bring with us into the world a nature which is untruthful, timid and irritable, but it cannot compel us to keep that nature. We *can* what we *will*, and karma will give a truthful, brave and gentle nature, if we set going the causes which produce it; karma is merely result, and as the one character is the inevitable result of certain causes, so is the other character the equally inevitable result if we choose to set going the appropriate causes.

We have seen that *desire makes opportunity*. We think carefully and quietly of the things which will be really useful to us, choosing the more permanent as against the less permanent, the intellectual and emotional as against the physical. Then we deliberately set ourselves to desire the most desirable objects. We desire them steadily, perseveringly, and we watch for the opportunities which our desire is making for us, and seize them as they present themselves. But let us remember that the law works unswervingly, and that we shall inevitably find falling into our hands the opportunity we have resolutely created, bringing with it the desired object. If ill-chosen, it will bring disappointment not satisfaction, sorrow not joy. Nature pays over results, indifferent to their nature, and it is for us to choose as we will. Hence the warning: *Take heed how ye pray*.

We have seen also that *action makes circumstances*, and that we lie in beds of our own making. A careful consideration of the relation between our character and our circumstances will teach us how best we may utilize the environment from which we cannot escape. While we diligently try to spread happiness round us, we should take advantage of the conditions to develop qualities we lack. From ill-health we may cull the sweet flowers of cheerfulness and patience; from household cares we may learn tenderness, and develop executive ability; from the drudgery of daily toil we may learn endurance; from anxiety we may evolve fortitude and serenity. The knower of karma turns everything to account and, like a strong and skillful workman, he shapes his future. Karma conditions us, but we are its creators, and in proportion to our knowledge is our control.

The little group of questions remaining is really answered in essence by what has been said, but we may run over certain additional details. "Are we the servants of karma, or its masters? Must we fold our hands meekly before it, or struggle vigorously against it? If today grows out of yesterday, and yesterday out of the day before, and so on, backwards and backwards, how can the bad man ever become good? are we not really compelled by an iron necessity?"

The first question of this group we may pass as already answered: we are partly servants, partly masters — servants by what remains in us of ignorance, masters by all the powers we gain by knowledge. The second question, however, raises an important point. Suppose we find ourselves in the grip of an overwhelming force and any struggle against it is doomed to failure, is there any use in struggling? Every use, as a little thought will show. Let us take a bad physical habit, brought over from the past — drunkenness or sexual sensuality. The man who does not understand karma, says despairingly: "I cannot help it," and he yields without a struggle, and thus weaves another strand into the rope of vice that binds him, making it stronger than before. The man who understands karma says: "It may be that I cannot help it, but I am going to fight against it for as long as I can, even if I have to succumb in the end." He makes a gallant fight against his enemy; beaten at last by the overwhelming force of his past, he sinks again into the vice; but his noble struggle has broken many strands of that strong rope of evil karma, and when again his foe assails him, the rope will bind him less securely, and he will be able to make a better fight, until — even though it be after many struggles and many defeats — the rope will snap, his limbs will be free, and he will slay his enslaver. When a man has created a vice by evil desire, evil thought, and evil act, he, its creator, can also be its destroyer, by good desire, good thought, and good act. Thread by thread the rope of karma is twisted; thread by thread the rope of karma may be untwisted; none but man himself creates his destiny, *none else compels* . Take courage, then, all ye who find your present tied and bound by your past; fear not, be of good courage, exert to the very utmost all the strength you have; and you shall inevitably free yourselves, and stand erect as masters where now you crawl as slaves. For law is law, and by the same law by which we bound ourselves shall we now assuredly free ourselves; the law remains the same, and that which in ignorance we wrought by it shall we now through knowledge undo by it, and none can say us nay.

The third question of this group is one which often seems to disturb the mind of the student; must not a vicious man, who continues to live viciously, come back in another life yet more vicious, and so on and on? There are certain counteracting forces which have to be considered. In the first place unhappiness follows on vice, to some extent in this world, to a great extent in the next. The drunkard, the sensualist, develop a bloated, coarsened body, with shaken nerves and ruined health. How often may such an one be heard to regret his folly, and to declare that if he could live his life over again, he would live it differently.

Experience teaches, in spite of our wilfulness, and the disregarded law bruises the evildoer. The suffering grows keener on the other side of death, as the scorpion of evil desire stings its nurturer, and the man is forced to recognize that he is living in a world of law, where he may dash himself against the barriers but cannot break them. When he passes from the intermediate world into the heavenly, every seed of good he has within him grows into flower; all that there is of pure and loving in him develops and increases: when the heaven-life is over, the good side of him is strengthened, his faculties are improved. On his return to earth he also brings with him the result of his sad experience as a shrinking from the evil in which before he delighted. The memory of suffering endured, burnt into the soul, has become a cause for avoidance of the evil which induced it, and thus, by the action of law, is a change brought about in the attitude of the man towards that particular vice. Again, humanity as a whole is slowly carried forward in the great current of evolution, and the evil-doer is carried with it, though he may retard his own progress, almost to the point of stationariness; but this wilful setting of a part against the whole, the insolent setting of the individual will against the universal, causes a friction that becomes intolerably painful, and at last ceases by the strong compulsion of this pain. Or again, the evil-doer reads a book, hears a discourse, meets a person, that arouses in him a recognition of the folly of the course he is pursuing, opens his eyes to the suffering he is creating for himself, and stirs his intelligence and his will into an effort to change. Or again, the disapproval of those he loves and honors, the wish to gain affection instead of incurring dislike, these act upon him as a new cause to cease from evil and to do good. Or yet again, the mere fact of his own growth, the unfolding, however slow, of the divine Spirit which is his deepest Self, inevitably quickens the inborn tendency to good and causes a struggle against evil. Man's tendency is upwards not downwards, and only by doing violence to his own nature can a man grovel in a dust-heap instead of walking with face uplifted to the sun.

"*Are we not really compelled by an iron necessity?*" There is but one necessity which binds the universe — the loving Will of its Emanator to raise it to perfection and bliss. As God's very Life is the life in His worlds, that Life lifts them ever to higher and fuller expression of Beauty, of Good, of Happiness. Evolution is the essence of that Will, and sooner or later, as the magnetized needle sets itself to the Pole, so must man's will set itself to the divine, whereof it is indeed a part. Man is at strife with himself, and hence the turmoil and the pain. When he sees his lasting happiness, the substance instead of the shadow, then will he be at one with himself and one with Divinity, and enter into the Peace.

BOOK FIVE
SOME KARMIC PROBLEMS

The Theosophical Review. Vol. 32

IN our early Theosophical days we grasped the broad idea of Karma, and it is only as we plunge more deeply into study that we discover the innumerable complexities in the working out of the Good Law; initial difficulties vanish as our vision clears, but new ones ever arise on the mental horizon, so that our ignorance seems to increase more rapidly than our knowledge.

In taking up some of these problems for study, we may assume that all Theosophists are acquainted with the three-fold division of Karma, and with the general workings of desire, thought and action.

The first type we may consider is an action which seems to be entirely out of relation to the character of the actor, as when a man of high character suddenly commits a crime. Such all action may be the result of a cause set going long ago in his past, a cause which has not found its opportunity of acting until many lives after the one in which it was generated. We have here an extreme instance of a general rule, that a man's actions often bear little relation to his present ideas. His actions are mostly the results of his desirings and thinkings in the past, modified but slightly by his desirings and thinkings in the present. A man is at one and the same time the reaper and the creator of Karma, and doing is reaping. As he acts he is sowing fresh seed for the future in his present desirings and thinkings, but the action as such is the harvest of past sowings; it is the outcome of the man as he was, not of the man as he is. To judge a man by his actions is to pass judgment on the man of the past, not on the man of the present; hence "Judge not" has been the maxim of the Teachers. None can judge a man aright, unless he can read his thoughts and desires, the outgrowth of his present character. Wide is the difference between our thoughts and our actions, our aspirations and our achievements. The thought comes from what we *are* at the present time, we create it according to the powers we have evolved; the action is fettered on all sides by its generating causes in the past, and is the manifestation of what we *were*.

The most startling discrepancies between present character and present actions arise in the more highly evolved types, and especially in persons whose evolution has been rapid.

In a far-off past a man has desired and thought an evil thing, and has completed it on the astral and mental planes (we will return to this in a moment). Now behind each man is a mass of mixed Karma, and only a certain amount of it can be worked out in any given personality. The Lords of Karma select out of this mixed mass such portions as are sufficiently congruous with each other to be worked out in a single type, within certain limitations of character and circumstances, and having regard to the persons in incarnation at the period of this particular man's life. The evil thing awaiting manifestation as action cannot find its opportunity for many lives — very possibly because the person or persons related to it do not take birth at the time when the man is on earth. Hence it is held over life after life. Meanwhile the man is making rapid progress, develops his character and strengthens all his powers. Yet this veritable sword of Damocles is suspended over his head, ready to fall. The opportunity for action comes at last, and the evil thing takes birth as an action. The saint sins, to the astonishment of himself and of those around him; and all men question: "Why is this? Surely his present strength should suffice to prevent such an act".

This brings us to the meaning of the phrase used above: "completed it on the astral and mental planes". An activity is composed of three stages — desire, thought, act; we wish for a thing (desire), we think how to obtain it (thought), we grasp it (act). During the first two stages we enjoy comparative freedom; as we are desiring, thought, prompted by experience, may step in and wrestle with the desire, may conquer and slay it, so that, that activity is stayed and does not pass on into the second stage. Or we may reach the second stage, and be thinking how to accomplish our desire, and other thoughts, again prompted by experience, may wrestle with this thought and overcome it, and the activity is stayed at the second stage. But when the second stage is completed, and the thought is ripe for action, so that only the open door of circumstance is needed for the thought to burst through it into action, then freedom is past, and the moment the door opens the act will be done.

Sometimes a wall of circumstances is built between the completed second stage and the third, and the action waits; death may come, but still the action waits, standing on the threshold until the door opens. Many lives may pass, and the door may not open; suddenly, in some life, circumstances open the door of opportunity, and the man performs the action without another thought, aye, though fifty or a hundred lives may have intervened. Such an action is inevitable, for its generating causes are complete, and, however incongruous it may be with the tenor of the life in which it occurs, it must come.

It must be remembered that the condition of the inevitableness of an action is that the desire and thought stages are *completed*. If there is a moment in which the man can think before he acts, if the action be not instinctive — done without thought — he can resist. There are all grades of difficulty in resisting the impulse to do a particular act, but wherever there is time to think there is power to resist.

It may not be amiss here to note the fact that if a man, who has some evil thing behind him awaiting birth as an act, be a man sufficiently evolved to remember his past, he may then destroy the evil Karma that waits on the threshold, he may burn up Karma by knowledge. For he can send against the completed thought a new current of thought of the opposite character and destroy the evil ere opportunity has manifested the thought as act. In this way also, where the act is connected with a person, an ancient enemy, the enemy may be turned into a friend by sending to him streams of good will ere the meeting on earth takes place, and the old hatred seeking revenge may be made love seeking to bless.

The great Teachers of the world, knowing this possibility, have ever inculcated universal love and goodwill, and by obedience to Them a man may transform an ancient foe into a friend, even though he knows not of his existence. For, taking it for granted that in his past he has generated some Karma of hatred, he may daily send out a wave of goodwill to all that lives, so that his love, outspreading in all directions, may quench any fires of hatred still fed by long-past wrongs.

Some interesting karmic problems arise in connection with World-Teachers, the Divine Men who come into the world for its helping. For instance, let us consider the "working of miracles" by the Founder of Christianity, miracles being, as we know, manifestations of the subtler forces on the physical plane.

The Karma generated by a miracle is of two kinds. First, there is the good done by it physically and mentally; secondly, there is the effect of the miracle on the minds of the onlookers. Such a manifestation of super-physical power usually convinces a number of the spectators of the authority of the person wielding the power; as time goes on, the miracle becomes more and more of a difficulty in their minds, until in the majority of cases it comes to be regarded as a trick or a hallucination, and resentment too often grows up against the Teacher, who is regarded as a deceiver. This evil thinking grows out of the act of the Teacher, since if He had not performed the miracle, the antagonism would not have been generated.

Yet it may be necessary for the Teacher to gain by such means a hearing for his Message; it may be necessary from the condition of the earth at the time, that there should be an exhibition of occult powers. Then the Messenger of the Great Lodge must, having undertaken the task, use the necessary means to win a hearing, and vindicate the reality of the invisible worlds, and hence, He generates this mixed Karma of good and evil, working on for hundreds of years. We can see in the modern revolt against miracles, due to what is called " the scientific spirit", the weapon against Christianity forged by that past necessity. What can the Teacher do? He must strike the balance between the good and the bad results, and do the action which brings the preponderance of good as its result. He must deliberately take on Himself the evil Karma as part of the sacrifice He makes in helping the world. And the way this Karma works is to bind Him to the movement He has started, and He must remain with His religion, guiding, loving, helping, until the Karma is exhausted that He generated in performing His work of salvation.

Many Messengers of the White Lodge, greater and lesser, have brought such reaction on themselves in the doing of the work — Mme. H. P. Blavatsky is a notable recent example. Out of this we may draw the general principle — one of the greatest practical importance — that no action done, in an imperfect world can be wholly good in its results.

"Every action is surrounded with evil as a fire is surrounded with smoke". No action that we can do is wholly good. All actions generate mixed Karma, because, being done in an imperfect world, the best must cause some friction, and we can only strive to choose the lines of work in which the good most preponderates. We must study the Law in order that we may understand its workings, and then in all our activities seek the balance of good, cheerfully bearing the inevitable evil which must accompany all the good we do.

Nor must we forget the goal to which the universe is tending. It bears as fruitage not only Divine Men, but within its matrix a LOGOS is evolving, who will be the builder of a higher universe. Great as a LOGOS is, He has climbed through all the forms — mineral, vegetable, animal, human, superhuman; and it is only because He has done this that He has acquired all-knowledge, and thus can begin a higher universe within the one in which He evolved. All the imperfect stages are necessary for the gaining of perfect knowledge, and what is a passing misery which produces an everlasting power? All the sufferings round us work to this end, as well as towards the evolution of each individual, and all the friction that occurs is caused by the continual growth. As we all evolve, the friction diminishes, and the Saviours in the later stages of evolution, being surrounded by more highly evolved beings, will have a better field to work in than had Those of the past, and thus less evil Karma will be generated in the doing of Their good work.

When we understand this part of the working of the Law, we can act with cheerfulness, using our best judgment, reason, thought, and all our experience, performing actions to the best of our ability , sure that some good and also some evil must result, but striving to maximize the good, to minimise the evil. In proportion as we reach this state of mind will our work be efficient, and we shall be able to see that while the Logos of the universe rules and guides all, among us also a Logos is evolving and we with Him. At every stage there is and must be imperfection, good and evil mixed, and all we can do is to cause as much good and as little evil as possible. To be troubled and regretful is to increase the friction which delays the total evolution, and anxiety can only throw fresh obstacles in the way. Brave cheerfulness is our right attitude, and as we advance we must grow more calm, peaceful, serene, contented, no matter what troubles may surround us. In the midst of the storm we may carry a heart of peace.

If we clear our eyes from personality; if we learn to identify ourselves with the Divine Man who is our Self; if we seek only God and the Law, indifferent to all our own circumstances; then the vision will become clearer and clearer, the mists will disappear, the path of right conduct will shine out, and even if sometimes we fail to tread it, the very failure will teach us to tread better in the future, for "Never doth one who worketh righteousness, O Beloved, tread the path of woe".

THE END.

Made in United States
Troutdale, OR
01/08/2025